STORIES OF ADOPTION:
LOSS AND REUNION

Eric Blau

FOREWORD BY ANNETTE BARAN

NEWSAGE PRESS

STORIES OF ADOPTION: LOSS AND REUNION

Address inquiries to NewSage Press,
825 N.E. 20th Ave., Suite 150, Portland, OR 97232

First Edition 1993

Printed in Korea through Print Vision,
Portland, Oregon.

ISBN 0-939165-17-1 (Softcover)

Library of Congress
Cataloging-in-Publication Data

Blau, Eric, 1947—
    Stories of Adoption: Loss and Reunion /
by Eric Blau; foreword by Annette Baran. —1st ed.

    p. cm

    ISBN 0-939165-17-1 : $16.95

    1. Adoptees—United States—Biography.
2. Birthparents—United States—Biography.
3. Adoptees—United States—Psychology.
4. Birthparents—United States—Psychology.

I. Title

HV875.55.B58 1993

362.7'34'092273—dc20   92-37504
[B]   CIP

Dedication

For my children
Kevin and Lauren

CONTENTS

FOREWORD

The pages within this extraordinarily moving volume offer, in photographic image and personal reflection, a rare opportunity for the reader to share the inner feelings of adoptees, birthparents, and adoptive parents. The men and women whom you will meet in *Stories of Adoption: Loss and Reunion* are of varying ages, backgrounds, and lifestyles, but they occupy similar emotional mazes, convoluted by the secrets, deceptions, and confusion characteristic of the adoption triangle. Many experience profound loss. The emotional amputation inherent in adoption is lifelong for adoptees and birthparents and affects their self-concept and self-worth to a significant degree.

Eric Blau has not only captured a special human essence in each of the photographs, but his interviews cut deeply into the individual's core. Some of the people are stoic and contained in their feelings; others express their grief, alienation, and anger in the most moving and explicit terms. Blau's images, both photographic and verbal, speak loudly. *Stories of Adoption* offers the reader a new understanding of a large group of people whose pain and suffering has not been sufficiently recognized.

Adoption, in some form, has been practiced since the beginning of society. It is universal, necessary, and valuable as a solution to a fundamental void. Throughout history, whenever dependent children have become kinless—without parents or other relatives—strangers have come forward to care for them.

Today, whether formal and legally enforced, or informal and unstructured, adoption still remains limited in scope and is not perceived as equal to biological membership in the family. In many older, more homogeneous societies, blood ties, family lineage, and class membership are of great importance. In many societies it is unthinkable to erase an individual's birthright. For those who must be reared by strangers, the dual identity is maintained—pride in heritage and root in family exist along with loyalty and love for the nurturing family.

In most of the world, adoption is still focused on children who need protection. In the United States, however, adoption developed very differently. The number of legal adoptions in this country is greater than in the rest of the world combined. Because of our melting-pot composition, we have placed our emphasis on achievement rather than background. In theory, our democratic foundation offered unlimited upward mobility. Our society encouraged us to believe that heredity was of no importance and that each individual could reach the highest goals. We were proud of our mixed ethnic composition and denied Old World strictures, which for centuries had kept people in their socio-economic cages. We, in the United States, in this century, overturned a practice centuries old and built a powerful legal institution of adoption. The men and women in this book offer testimony to the results of the American experiment in secret, anonymous adoption practices.

Adoption was a perfect fit in this new world. In the early years of the Colonies, orphaned children were brought over from England to work the farms and provide a cheap, ready labor force. These children, absorbed into rural families, often took on new names and identities, although without legal sanction or inheritance rights. As the country grew, national groups such as the Child Welfare League were formed to set standards and provide safeguards. Legal adoption followed as a further step to insure stability, security, and inheritance rights for the children.

There was no thought, in those pioneer days, of sealing records, hiding the identity of the birth family, or pretending the child was not adopted. Not until the focus moved from meeting the needs of children to those of infertile couples were such procedures contemplated. Trying to keep the fact of adoption a secret was attempted for many decades but failed; too many people knew or suspected the truth and were apt to gossip. Because adoptees were often taunted in a punitive and humiliating manner, adoptive parents promised to tell the child the truth. In fact, many adoptees are told that they are special and better because they were given up out of love by their birthparents and chosen by their adoptive parents.

Many infertile couples applying to adopt became convinced, with the help of adoption social workers, that heredity was of little importance compared to environment, that adoption would overcome their infertility because there was no difference between giving birth and adopting a child. To try to make it the same, all the original information was erased, destroyed, or sealed, and a whole new identity, that of the adopting family, was given to the child.

For the great majority of couples, adoption is an option taken only after failure to have their own biological offspring. It is a second choice at best and a last resort for many, facts that become inoperative when the adoptive placement occurs. Even though the adoptive parents are overjoyed after years of disappointment, when they finally become parents, paradoxically, the child is supposed to feel grateful and fortunate to have been adopted by them. In this equation, birthparents are told that they have come to a resolution of their problem when they relinquish their child. They are told, "The problem is solved, your feelings are dealt with, and you need never think about that child again."

Unfortunately, human beings' emotions are not subject to formulae, devised by others. Legal court action does not seal feelings, only original birth certificates. Adoption is a lifelong problem with many layers of complexity that cannot be cured with simplistic cliches and solutions.

Birthparents do not resolve their feelings when they sign away their children. They continue to grieve. Many adoptive parents also silently grieve. They live with the ghosts of the birthparents, whom they fear their children really love. Often they secretly perceive their adopted children as different and alien and feel that they never really fit into the family constellation. Moreover, many adoptive parents compare their adoptive children unfavorably to the children they imagine they would have given birth to. Adoptees, in this triangular web of emotions, tend to be vulnerable to the feeling that there is something wrong with them that led to their being "dumped," abandoned, given away. They fantasize about their origins; the birthmother might be either a fairy princess or, conversely, a whore. Adoptees often feel different from their adoptive parents and other relatives in appearance, personality, interests, and intelligence—and in some instances unacceptable.

The emotional need for information, contact, or reunion exists for most adoptees and birthparents. However, until recently, these visceral feelings have been denied and repressed as unacceptable by both parties because of all the secrecy and anonymity surrounding the adoption. Nevertheless, there have always been some intrepid individuals who secretly searched for and found each other and were reunited.

Within the past twenty-five years, however, a major revolution has taken place. The traditional practice of "closed adoption" has been challenged and is no longer considered acceptable in current adoption placements. Legislation is being introduced to open old sealed records, but neither adoptees nor birthparents are willing to wait. Illegal but highly effective underground routes exist for birthparents and adoptees that provide the necessary information. Nothing, it turns out, is that secret or anonymous. More adoptees and birthparents are searching for and finding one another with the help of local and national organizations that lobby on their behalf and provide support networks.

Historically, adoption has been highly romanticized and imbued with sentimentality, pathos, and unfulfilled desires. It is, in reality, an imperfect and seriously flawed institution that needs reevaluation and restructuring. The men and women whom you will meet in the ensuing pages offer deep testimony to the emotional voids they feel, largely due to having relinquished a child or having been that relinquished child. Although reunion does not compensate for the lost decades and is often an incomplete or even unhappy event, it is a necessary step in the right direction. Reunion solves the mysteries, answers questions, and provides closure to a greater or lesser degree for the individuals involved.

Currently old adoption records are still sealed in all but two states, Alaska and Kansas. However, the trend in new adoptive placements are more or less "open." Birthparents, recognizing how valuable their unborn infants are in a marketplace where there are many more infertile couples and fewer and fewer babies, are insisting on choosing the families for their children. The range of continuing openness in adoptive placement varies greatly, from minimal meetings between the adoptive parents and birthparents prior to placement to ongoing contact throughout the years. A fundamental change, however, is the absence generally of the promise of secrecy and anonymity.

In the future, if records are no longer sealed, and if adoptive placements are open with continued access for all parties, searches and reunions will be largely unnecessary. For the present, we have millions of adoptees and millions of birthparents who wonder and wait. We have others who find ways of circumventing the closed system, breaking codes, and effecting reunions. Most of the individuals in this book belong to that group; although Blau can only offer us a sample, they form a clear representation of the many faces of the adoptive experience.

Annette Baran

INTRODUCTION

Our lives don't begin with our birth, or even our conception. We are born into a complex tapestry, connected by threads running in many directions; we are shaped by our surroundings, by the background, the dynamics of the composition. The threads that support the design alternately emerge and dive behind an integral but invisible support. We find ourselves in a family and a culture. There are images, stories, home places, photographs, the family tree, flesh and blood.

One of photography's most compelling impacts on society has been providing people with permanent images of themselves and their loved ones. Photography has reached most deeply into the lives of individuals through these personal images. Family photographs, even the old ones, have a presence, a looking out beyond time and connecting with the world through that image surface. You might say, "Dead and gone", but you can still look these relatives in the eye, see them in their time and in yours. The connection, the person's presence, remains intact. In our complex and changing twentieth-century history, photographs of family are often the most tangible heritage. There is the resemblance, the shape of the face, the hazel eyes of Aunt so-and-so.

The adopted are a break in the thread. We are a hole in the fabric, surrounded by love and care, but we just don't fit into that shape, that outline. Everyone's life ties back into family, flesh, resemblance, and history. The adoptee doesn't have these and knows the surrogate threads are there more for convention and support than in fact. I remember people telling me how much I looked like my mother, my adoptive mother. I often wondered, "Would I know my true mother if I passed her on the street? My siblings, if we sat next to each other on a flight?"

Family photographs at one point played a significant role in my work. As a graduate student I'd haunt flea markets for old family albums and photographs. At home, I'd raid the family supply. I recombined all these images into collages that spoke to a sense of connection. It was a couple of years before I became conscious that I was not just involved with the artistic endeavor of surrealism, but in an unconscious way was constructing a familylike tree of images and faces that were longed for and missing in my real life. That my photographs could lead me to this unconscious yearning was one of the most powerful realizations my work has brought me.

The photographs, the stories, the connections—these are what the adoptee misses most deeply. Often the first questions asked of a rediscovered birthparent are about heritage. The most critical questions about birthparents may be about medical history, but the deepest questions, harder to articulate, are: What did they look like? What were their names? What are their stories?

Parents, 1987, Linda Connor

To search for and find one's birthparents is an act of incredible courage only made possible by compelling curiosity. The terrors felt in those encounters, after the years of uncertainty, curiosity, and fear, are at the very core of one's being. It's like having one's umbilical cord suddenly yanked, leaving one fighting for breath and bearings. What I imagined as a reunion of the sweetest nature, a celebration of life, was at least initially as traumatic as the birth and original separation.

Imagine calling your mother for the first time. Walking up to her door and having it open. Looking for the first time at her face, the face you have tried so very hard to conjure from your own. When I was 42 I found and met my birthmother for the first time. She didn't look like me. I wouldn't have known her if we had passed on the street.

That Eric Blau is a doctor as well as a photographer is evident in the compassion and interest he brings to his subjects in *Stories of Adoption: Loss and Reunion*. In all of these photographs, there's a sense of respect for the dignity of each person photographed. I don't feel the heavy artistic hand imposing a stylistic or formulaic approach. The primary subject of the photograph remains the person; Blau doesn't have a visual mold within which he constricts each subject. His portraits give forth a sense of "This is me"; they project the identity of the sitter strongly. The rooms and environments further amplify their lifestyles, the way they pull life around themselves, order it. The individuals in this book are ordinary people, yet I'm sure none of them feels ordinary.

Viewing family albums, particularly as a child, is part of a storytelling process in which the individual images serve as triggers for or landmarks in narratives about the family's past. How riveting it is to integrate the images and the stories in this book in a process similar to looking at the family album. The stories overlaid on these individuals and the sense we are given of how they have constructed their environments make us aware once again of how unique and powerful every human life is. Every person must construct an identity; however, for adoptees it is a more fragile, demanding task with far fewer givens, fraught with mystery. The compelling combination of photographs and true stories are what resonate so strongly in *Stories of Adoption*. Each story goes into my heart. I wonder how a nonadopted person feels reading these stories and looking at these photographs. Interest? Curiosity? Compassion? I felt a clutching at my core.

Linda Connor

PREFACE

Before I began working on this book, I must confess I knew little about adoption or the "adoption triangle"—adoptees, birthparents, and adoptive parents. Like most people outside the adoption triangle, I did not realize that millions of people are intimately involved with adoption, whether as adoptees, birthparents, or adoptive parents. I accepted many commonly held beliefs that adoptees were "lucky" to have been adopted and that the adoption system—in place for decades—worked well for all concerned. Mostly, I didn't think much about the issues surrounding adoption. But then I heard Mary's story.

Mary, who was adopted at birth, rented a spare room in a friend's home while attending graduate school at a local university. One day she received a phone call from her birthmother, who wanted to meet her. I was surprised by the myriad of emotions Mary felt. She was excited by the prospect of meeting her birthmother and half-sisters but fearful of the familial responsibilities that this reunion might entail. And for the first time in her life, she expressed anger that her birthmother had given her up for adoption. At the same time, Mary also felt guilty because she thought she might somehow betray her adoptive family by exploring a relationship with her biological family. Soon Mary began having fantasies that her birthmother was going to supplant her adoptive family as a source of support and guidance.

I found the range and complexity of Mary's emotions compelling, especially because they occurred even before meeting her birthmother. Although I knew families that adopted children, as well as birthparents who had given up infants for adoption, I was totally ignorant of the concerns that color their life experiences and often subvert their attempts to reconcile their pasts. I began talking with people who were part of the adoption triangle, and my education unfolded. I learned of the political and social movements spawned by them and the often incompatible goals these groups have. The aspect that was most interesting to me was the issue of adopted children and their birthparents being reunited. This event seemed to conjure up the most disparate and conflicting emotions. By design, all the people who tell of their lives in *Stories of Adoption: Loss and Reunion* have been involved in reunions.

In this book, the efforts of adoptees and their birthparents to meet one another serve as a catalyst to highlight these many conflicts. Paramount are those that balance birthparents' rights of privacy and the adoptees' right to know their genetic family's background. It is ironic that at a time when organized birthparents and adoptees are struggling for legislation that opens up the adoption process, there are many others in the adoption triangle that adamantly refuse to meet their relatives. Because this book focuses on reunion, these adoptees are not represented.

Stories of Adoption: Loss and Reunion offers autobiographies of people willing to tell their stories. I wonder what additional information might have been garnered from all those who declined my invitations for interviews. There were various reasons for their not participating in the book; some people were fearful of hurting relatives by admitting past indiscretions publicly. And in a few instances, individuals chose not to be in the book after they had been interviewed and photographed, deciding their stories were still too painful and some details still unknown by their families. There were also adoptees who stated emphatically that they were content with their lives and had no desire to pursue a reunion with birthparents. For them, traditional, closed adoption has worked fine. Despite their declining to be interviewed, I feel most of these people would agree that their points of view are well represented in this book.

I am grateful to the many people who spoke to me openly about the personal details of their lives. Too often autobiographies are for personal propaganda, not truth, but on the following pages these individuals tell their stories candidly, frequently exposing painful segments of their lives to public scrutiny. Collectively, these vignettes contain important information that will help us learn more about the multifaceted, imperfect institution of adoption.

Eric Blau

STORIES OF ADOPTION:
LOSS AND REUNION

"Adoption has a past, present, and future tradition. If you look at the story of Moses, it shows how adoption has an important role in developing the human aspects of people—compassion, love, and forgiveness."

Rebecca Leverant, adopted

PHILIP DRENTH

was adopted at birth and had a strict, religious upbringing along with an older sister who was also adopted. In his mid-20s, Drenth, now 30, searched for and found his birthmother.

When I searched, I didn't know what I was going to find. My curiosity was really going. At the same time, emotionally, I didn't expect any great orchestral overtures in my life as a result of it. As a matter of fact, I was annoyed by these people that would think, "Oh, you're looking for your mother, you're damaged." I felt really incensed by that attitude. However, for the most part, I didn't encounter too much of that, although I did get it at the hospital where I was born.

At the very beginning of the search I was 25. I started searching at the prodding of an old girlfriend, but I didn't really make a project of it until I was 27. Initially, I was curious to find out for myself what the difference was between genetics and environment in creating a person, and what better way to find out than to investigate myself? Had the effort been continuous, I would have found my birthmother within two weeks. Because I needed to prepare myself mentally for the impact of the next step of the process, I took it one step at a time over the course of a year.

I had a fantasy of what meeting my birthmother would be like. I guess I should preface it by saying that I'd always felt really starved for any kind of mentor. My adoptive father was aloof. I'd see him go off to work in the morning and come back at night. I never knew much about a man's duties while growing up. In my late teens and 20s it was, "What are you going to do for the rest of your life? What are you going to do for a career?" All this pressure, and I didn't have any answers. So, in the back of my mind, I was thinking that we'd meet at a fairly nice place for a beverage, my birthmother would be in a smart business suit, and she'd be that mentor. That wasn't exactly how it turned out.

My birthmother and I met at a diner on the east end of town, about ten miles from the Texas border. I walked in and I saw this woman sitting over at a table, and we could tell from the eye contact that we were each other. I was overwhelmed. I had so much curiosity, but once I sat down and I got a cup of coffee, I didn't know what to say. I've never been great at conversations—I think I'm bad—and she was not much help. We kind of fumbled for awhile. After an hour and a half, we went over to a bar where my birthmother had worked as a bartender until recently. We both had five drinks. After about the second or third drink, she started loosening up and I felt like I could breathe. After that we went over to her trailer and continued talking. She was really worried that I'd be disappointed with who I'd found. Sometimes the facts don't turn out like you'd expect, but that doesn't mean they're the wrong facts. I was there two days, and it was one intense emotion after another. Every emotion I could possibly imagine, all compacted into one big, complex, multifaceted thing.

As I get to know my birthmother and the rest of the family, different realizations fall out. I'd say the most important one is that she is really proud of me. By the time we got to the bar that first night, less than two hours after we met, my birthmother was introducing me to everyone as, "This is my boy who has come out from California to see me."

"My birthmother and I met at a diner on the east end of town, about ten miles from the Texas border. I walked in and I saw this woman sitting over at a table, and we could tell from the eye contact that we were each other."

Months later, I realized she was really happy with who she found. She was proud of me. That soaked in through my pores, without me realizing it. Growing up, my adoptive parents were devout Christian people. I felt like I was getting all this religion rammed down my throat, and there was no discussion of it. I remember feeling burdened by my parents' egos. I was told, "Be A, not B. You should be this, not that." I knew I was the symbol of my adoptive parents' disappointment. Although my parents didn't consciously do it, or maliciously do it, still I felt that burden. Finding my roots gave me a sense of self-worth.

I try to avoid comparisons between my birthmother and my adoptive mother, but in one area my birthmother really gives me the mentorship I'd been searching for. She gives me great support and advice about my love life. When I'm making mistakes she chuckles and clues me in to what I'm doing wrong. She helps me see things from a woman's perspective. My adoptive mom, by contrast, is downright destructive. She's so full of fear that every piece of advice amounts to "Something's bound to go wrong"; "Don't take any risks"; "She isn't your type"; or "She's only being nice to you because she wants something." I remember growing up being afraid of these monsters because of stories my adoptive mother would tell about how when you get women alone they'll scream "Rape!" I'm grateful to my birthmother for just being who she is. Of course women are not monsters, and my birthmother has helped me understand the social language, not filtered through the filter of fear and possessiveness. I understand the meanings of people's behaviors so much better now, and I feel much more integrated into the world around me. Now that I understand the language of the people around me, I know how to get the things I want in my life. I thank my birthmother for her vital contribution.

I discovered my birthfather's name, but I haven't made any special effort to find him because I've gone out with women who know what it feels like to be pregnant and abandoned. I understand their feelings, and if I ever met my father, I'd get the information I wanted from him and let him know that it doesn't matter how ignorant he was of the hurt he caused my birthmother or what his intentions were, the results are still the same. I've gone out with too many women who were full of hurt because of guys like that. While I understand their distrust of men in general, I see no reason not to pound spikes through the hearts of the sources of that pain, even if they weren't the ones specifically responsible. You don't just dispose of people once you're "done" with them just because they're no longer convenient. But if that's the status quo you set, then you'd better be willing to take your turn on the cross.

The ability to find your birthparents is fundamental. I feel in my bones that if we have any rights at all, the right to a sense of history is fundamental. It's a foundation that you can build on. However, my sister feels very threatened by searching for her birthparents and would never do what I've done. But I'm not my sister, and this is something that I needed to do. There are so many people in this world who try to limit other people with their fears, especially adoptive parents. I think it's very selfish because the only thing they're thinking about is their own emotions. Children are not chattel, any more than spouses are. I'm not just a manifestation of someone else's family line into eternity.

Philip Drenth

SHARRON LEE gave up her newborn daughter, Debbie, for adoption when she was 21 years old. Lee later married and had a son. In her early 30s, after learning she had a degenerative eye disease that could be worsened by another pregnancy, she adopted Kelly. When Kelly was about 9, Lee searched for and found Debbie, who was then 18. When Kelly was 17, Lee assisted in her adopted daughter's search for her birthparents. Kelly found both her birthparents and regularly visits with them. Lee also sees her daughter Debbie regularly._

Giving my daughter Debbie up for adoption was definitely an intellectual decision. There were many times that I seriously considered keeping Debbie. Basically it was probably more my parents' decision than it was mine. There was tremendous family pressure to give Debbie up for adoption. I can remember calling my parents in the middle of the night and saying, "I decided to keep the baby." They told me, "You are not keeping the baby." I just caved in because what was I going to do? I hadn't graduated yet and what was I going to do with the baby? Particularly since society at that time was so disapproving. It was all very hush-hush and secret. I was even living under an assumed name.

Once Debbie was born, I was so relieved. The whole nightmare was over with and I had really anticipated feeling a loss, which I didn't feel. I think I was feeling, "Let me out of here. Let me go back and resume my life. I don't want any more of this, and I have had it." During the pregnancy it was one lie after another, and I was anxious to get on with my life and start having fun again. I think I buried a whole lot of feelings at that point in time.

I think if abortion had been open to me at that time, I definitely would have had one. I was cut off from everything. Today there is a totally different attitude in society. But at that time, I was totally alone. Plus, those first couple of months of pregnancy when you are not making any connection with that child, it would have been easier to abort. But the latter months of pregnancy are a whole different ball game. You feel that baby moving, and you are bonding with that child before it is born. I did a lot of deep burying of feelings at that time, probably out of self-preservation. Probably some good counseling could help those feelings surface.

There is a nice closeness now in my relationship with Debbie without it being a smothering one. I don't feel like her mother—I never have and I never will. But there definitely is a real interest and a warmth beyond just a friendship. I don't feel for Debbie what I feel for Kelly and my son.

Basically, the reason that my husband and I decided to adopt Kelly was because shortly after our son was born I found out that I had a degenerative eye disease, which had not been diagnosed prior to his birth. This disease is hereditary, and at that time there had been so little research done on it, there was a belief that possibly my pregnancy was contributing to the progression of the eye disease. So rather than take the chance of passing the disease on, we decided that we would adopt. We had our son, and so we wanted to adopt a girl. I can honestly say I don't think there was a tie-in between my giving up Debbie and wanting to adopt a girl. If our son had been a girl, we would have adopted a boy, so I don't think that was a contributing factor. But after we adopted Kelly, probably a year later, it really hit me, and I did go for some counseling. I got out all my anger and

"The thing I really would like to see overcome around adoption is the reluctance of adoptive parents to let their adopted children meet their birthparents. If anything, with Kelly, meeting her birthparents has improved our relationship."

all the bottled-up feelings toward my parents for having made me give my daughter up for adoption. I think I really dealt with the grief for the first time eleven years later.

I think one of the reasons that Kelly has presented so many challenges to us is because her inborn temperament is so totally different from the rest of the family. Kelly is very impulsive, and she has always been impulsive, and we never quite knew where Kelly was coming from. My husband and my son and myself are totally the opposite, so trying to bridge that gap between the way our personalities interacted with Kelly's personality presented some problems. How much do you attribute to the adoption and how much to genetics? I don't know, but we have worked through the challenges very well.

The thing I really would like to see overcome around adoption is the reluctance of adoptive parents to let their adopted children meet their birthparents. I know from listening to talk shows and from reading that there are still an awful lot of adoptive parents out there who are still terribly threatened by this. Reunion doesn't weaken your relationship with your kid. If anything, with Kelly, meeting her birthparents has improved our relationship. Kelly's knowing who she is certainly hasn't changed anything in our relationship. I know she considers me as her mom, and her dad is her dad no matter what. Even with as much contact as Kelly has with her birthparents, we are her family, and we will always be her family.

Sharron Lee

My family is the people with whom I live—my adoptive mom and dad, who raised me, and my brother. I have one brother, and I have half-brothers and half-sisters. Knowing my birth family hasn't affected that at all. I don't go to my birthfather and say, "Give me ten dollars for the weekend." My family is my adoptive parents. These are the people I live with. These are the people I talk about my problems with.

But I do spend time with my birth family too. My birthfather and I visit my paternal grandmother because she likes to spend a lot of time with me and catch up on what she has missed. Since my birthfather has two younger children, I baby-sit a lot for them, and I watch their house when they go out of town. It is not like he is my father, we are more friends. I put Sharron Lee, my adoptive mother, in her place as my mother. I put my birthmother in her place as my friend and a little bit more. We have a lot more ties than just normal friends would have, but our relationship can't go any further than that.

My birthmother had called my adoptive mom and told her that she was not doing a proper job because at the time I had a boyfriend, and she didn't agree with things I was doing, and my adoptive mom did. I came home and my adoptive mom was crying. I said, "No one tells you that you were wrong. No one ever questions you. I don't question you." I called my birthmother and told her that she was wrong in doing that. My adoptive mom and my birthmom had a really good relationship until then, and they would talk on the phone almost every day. But not after that. I freaked out, and I couldn't believe that my birthmom did that.

My birthmother and I are close. We go out to lunch and do fun things, but I know that if our relationship got too close again, that it could endanger other relationships that are more important to me. My birthmother is my natural mother, and that is fine. I'm glad I met her, but I won't let it take away from the relationship between me and my adoptive mother, my mom, my mommy. If I had to choose whether I would meet my birthparents or stay with my adoptive family and be happy not knowing my birthparents, I would choose my adoptive family. If it was going to endanger my family, I wouldn't meet my birthparents. I would be satisfied with my life.

Kelly Lee

STEPHANIE MELLO

was adopted as an infant. Mello, who is biracial, was adopted by a white family. When she was 15, she had a successful reunion with her birthmother, which was the first time she had been exposed to African-American people and culture. When Mello was 16 she decided she wanted to meet her birthfather, but when she first contacted him, he was unwilling to meet her. With help from her adoption therapist, Mello met her birthfather when she was 21. Although her birthfather ultimately became interested in her, her reunion with him was not as satisfying as her reunion with her birthmother. Mello feels her adoptive parents are very open-minded; however, she wishes they would have given her more exposure to black culture.

I don't think being adopted ever really bothered me when I was growing up. I don't even think I noticed it. At one point I thought everybody was adopted. When I grew older and considered having children, I was going to adopt. I assumed I would adopt children. Then my mom said, "Why wouldn't you want to have a kid? You could have your own children." I thought, "It's not supposed to be that way, is it?" I had to recondition my thinking.

When I was young, I don't ever remember having fantasies about my birthparents or having inquired about them. I think I really felt my adoptive mom was my birthmom. I remember asking, "What did it feel like when I was in your belly?" She laughed for about five minutes because I had forgotten that I was adopted. You'd think it would be hard to forget because my adoptive mom and dad are white, and I am biracial. But somehow, I'd forget. Color didn't mean anything to me then. I didn't start having fantasies until after I was told at the age of 15 who my birthmother was. I had to wait a whole week before I could meet her, and during that time I had fantasies about how wonderful and perfect she would be. Over time, however, I became very disappointed. She was not what I thought a mother should be like, and my expectations were unrealistically high. I had to learn to accept my birthmother the way she was and vice versa.

My adoptive mom figured out who my birthmother was when I was 11, but she waited to tell me, which was good. If she had told me when I was 11, I think I might have been influenced too much, or unable to handle the disappointment correctly. At age 15, I had my own values and morals down, and a pretty good sense of who I was and what I was about. It was a better time.

When I first met my birthmother, I tried to trivialize our meeting as much as I could. On the meeting day, I went to school and kept telling myself, "It's no big deal, it's like I'm meeting a friend." A trait of mine is trying to make things as small as possible. Of course, I didn't even sleep the night before. At school I couldn't concentrate the whole day. On the way home, I got off the bus further down the line. We lived on Third Street, and I got off at Fourth. My adoptive mom and my birthmom were at the front window waiting for me to walk up Third, and I came up Fourth behind them. I jumped in the door and said, "Hi, I'm home," and just walked right up to her and said, "Hi, I'm Stephanie." I was totally casual about the whole thing. My birthmother, however, was standing there staring at me with her big wide eyes tearing up, and I'm thinking, "Oh, please, don't do that to me." The first thing I asked was, "Is that your real hair?" I had this curly, massively nappy hair, and my mom never knew what to do with it. So I looked at my

*"I had no problems
with my adoptive
mom when I met my
birthmother. I'm very
secure with her, and
we know where we
stand with each other,
and we love each
other."*

birthmother, and the first thing I noticed was this gorgeous straight hair that I always wanted, and I asked, "Is that your hair?" She looked at me and rolled her eyes and said it was a wig.

I had no problems with my adoptive mom when I met my birthmother. I'm very secure with her, and we know where we stand with each other, and we love each other. Adoptive parents seem to get jealous or hurt when they feel their relationships with their children aren't secure. They don't trust the child's love for them, therefore the birthparents are a threat. There's no reason for you to be fearful about your child meeting her birthparents if you trust in your relationship. My adoptive father and I are not so secure, and he felt left out and became a little jealous. We were not as tight growing up as my mom and I. He didn't understand that no one could ever take his place. My past is part of me, and no one has the right to rob me of a reunion because of their insecurities. That would be selfish and unfair. I did come from someone else, and I have the right to know from who. Pretending otherwise would be a lie.

When I first wrote to my birthfather, he didn't respond. I wrote more letters trivializing everything, saying, "It's no big deal, I just want to meet you. I don't want anything from you, no money, no support, I don't want to be part of your life, I don't want to meet your kids, I just want to meet you and see what you look like and act like. Why are you making such a big deal of this? Why won't you write back?"

After that, I got a call from the adoption agency that dealt with me when I was a kid. They said he had contacted them and did not want to have any contact with me. There was some crisis in his family at that time, and he didn't want me to pursue him any further. He also sent my birthmother a letter, getting very upset that she had provided some information to me. He threatened to sue her as "clearly and unequivocally as possible." My birthfather was a lawyer and sounded just like one. At first I was very mad, but then I felt the pain. I'd had this wonderful successful reunion with my birthmother, and she was terrific, so I assumed my birthfather would react the same way. I ended up feeling very rejected by my birthfather. I was 16 at the time. When I was 20, I thought that my birthfather's "life crisis" had gone on a little too long. I called him at work and said, "I'm Stephanie Mello, your birthdaughter. Do you have a few minutes?" He froze for about ten seconds. I said I wanted to meet him, and he said he thought "maybe one day we could do that." I was put off by him again.

Finally I wrote him a letter saying, "This time while I'm on the East Coast, I've promised myself I would meet you." I didn't mean it to sound threatening, but if that's what it was going to take, then I was glad I had pushed the right buttons. I felt bad because I knew he was afraid I was going to show up on his doorstep. He didn't know me; I could have been a psycho. I gave him my adoption therapist's phone number in that letter, and he called her immediately. I liked having a mediator. You can't do it alone. You need to have a trained mediator who knows how to deal with these things. He finally came to a meeting.

My birthfather was forty minutes late, and he was pissed off. He was nervous, too, I could tell, and he just didn't want to be there. I came wearing a little pro-fessional outfit, and I had ten pages of questions all written out, one to 100. I sat down with my pen and pencil, very formal, very stoic. I was going to take his little deposition and say, "Thank you very much, good-bye." I was going to be very cold and professional and not let him even think that I wanted him in my life. Again, I tried to make the meeting no big deal. I started interviewing him. "How was it you met my mother? What were the circumstances?" After the fifth or sixth question, I just started asking things, and I forgot my list. His eyes lifted from looking down on the floor, and he started studying me. He was getting curious. Around question number twenty, he started asking questions back. I got excited that he was taking interest. Then I asked, "Would you have ever wanted to meet me if I hadn't pushed you to?" He said, "I don't think so." I just ran out of the room to the bathroom next door and took five minutes to bawl by myself. Then I came back totally composed, but I was very, very upset.

The meeting was strange. My birthfather came in mad, but he didn't want to leave. He'd say he had to go, but then he'd ask more questions. When he did leave, I put out my hand to give him a good handshake, but instead, he gave me a kiss on the cheek. It was weird, very weird.

When I met my birthmother, black people were a curiosity to me. I remember meeting my birthmother and my brother and my grandmother. My birthmother said, "Wow, you've never really been around black people, have you?" She'd crack jokes or say certain things that I didn't understand. When I went to college I had a black roommate. The system assumes you're going to get along with someone of your own race, so

"When I met my birth-mother, black people were a curiosity to me....I never used to feel different in a white setting, but now that I'm getting more in touch with the black part of me, I do notice when I'm the only black person in a place."

they set me up with a black roommate. I'd argue with her and her black friends, but I learned a lot from her. We became pretty good friends, but I felt uncomfortable when we'd go to black clubs or all-black places. I felt out of place. I felt like a white person in a black setting. I didn't understand them. Why were they expecting me to be a certain way? They knew immediately that I was raised in a white town. I can go and function at a white bar or club in any town and feel OK. Ideally though, I love going to mixed places where there are both black and white people. I feel really at home in a mixed place. I never used to feel different in a white setting, but now that I'm getting more in touch with the black part of me, I do notice when I'm the only black person in a place. I never used to notice it. Never.

Now I'm going to Howard University in D.C., which is an all-black college, because I got sick of the fact that I wasn't comfortable around black people. I decided to throw myself into the situation and just learn. People there ask, "Why are you dating a white guy?" I hear people say, "I'd never date one." I hear that all the time. My response is, "One what? One human being? One person who's a shade different than you?" As if whites are a different species or something. I feel more comfortable with them because I grew up around them and understand whites better. My father is white. One person I met at college who is mixed-race like me, who also had white adoptive parents, told me, "You're gonna have to pick. Do you want to be black, or do you want to be white?" And I said, "You've got to be kidding. I'm not going to deny either half, babe." We didn't like each other.

One thing I'm angry about is that my adoptive mom didn't really show me books on black leaders or black ethnicity or culture. I think it would have been important for her to show me where I was from. I was told I was part Ethiopian and Cherokee Indian and white. It would have been nice to bring home some books from the library or expose me to black cultural things, though looking back, I wonder if I would've been interested. My adoptive mom is very open-minded and liberal, and she ended up just treating me like a person, not a color. When she adopted me, I think she just thought of who needed to be adopted the most. I feel like I wasn't prepared for the realities of the world, and I'm trying hard to deal with my "blackness" now.

I think I grew up with those values. I remember looking for a cat, and I went to this place where there were free cats. There were all these beautiful, pudgy kitties and one oversized striped cat that I knew wasn't going to be taken home because all the kids thought he wasn't cute. I picked him because I thought he wouldn't have a home. My adoptive mom thinks like that. There were a lot of black children to be adopted, and there weren't many white families who would do that.

When you're adopted, you feel like you were just placed with a family. You don't feel like you have roots. A lot of people don't understand that roots are a piece of you, that you were brought into a world by two people. For people who haven't been adopted, it's so hard for them to understand why meeting birthparents is so important. I'd ask them, "Wouldn't you want a little family history to know where you came from so you can feel rooted in the ground?"

Adoptees need to stand up for themselves to their adoptive parents. "If you love me and respect me, you should let me find my birthparents, just so I know who they are." Most adoptive parents don't understand this need. They feel threatened. They feel it's "unnecessary." But that's selfish. It may be unnecessary for them. Reunions are going to help adoptees understand themselves better, to feel stronger and more confident.

I think birthparents should be required to register somewhere to facilitate meeting their children. It should be an obligation on their part just to meet their children. I would balance the birthparents' right to privacy with the adoptive child's right to know by this meeting, like the one I had with my birthfather. I don't think he owes me anything else, but he did bring me into this world, so I think for me to ask for one meeting is not asking too much. Morally, that's how I think it should be.

Stephanie Mello

JOY TERAN

was adopted at birth by her birthmother's neighbor, who was also a friend. Teran first learned she was adopted at age 8. At 11, her adoptive parents divorced, and when Teran was 13, her adoptive mother died. She was placed in a foster home briefly and then lived with her adoptive father and his new wife. At 16, Teran graduated from high school and was again placed in a foster home because she was considered "uncontrollable." Teran was 21 when her birthmother contacted her and she met her two half-sisters. Teran, 31, is now divorced and has two children.

When I was 8 my mom just said, "I need to have a talk with you," and sat down and told me I was adopted. I remember not thinking that much of it—I don't think I really understood at 8 years old what it meant. I thought,"This is still my mom and my dad, and so what?" I didn't feel any different. I wasn't aware of being different till I got older. Now that I am aware, I look back at this time, and I see it made a great deal of difference because everyone in my parents' family, at least on my mother's side, knew that I was adopted and wasn't part of their family, and they treated me differently. As a child, I didn't really notice that. But as an adult, when I looked back I could see that it explained certain things.

Sometimes I would ask my mother questions about my birthmother. I remember her comment always being that my mother was a whore or prostitute or bad thing, and when she got mad at me she would say, "You're going to be just like your mother."

Prior to my birthmom finding me, I had never had any strong desire to look for my birthparents. I often heard adoptees saying that they've always wanted to know, but I never had. My birthmother called my ex-boyfriend's house, and he called me and said, "I just got a call from somebody who said she's your mother. Her name was Virginia." Well, one of the few things I knew about my mother was that her name was Virginia. So I was immediately blown away. I wasn't overjoyed, I was stunned, shocked. It was almost like a dream. Here was something I had never even imagined, or dreamed about. When we met, we talked about all this stuff, and she told me her side of the story, which of course I had never heard before. I had heard little bits and pieces, and I had been trying to put things together for years. It felt really good. I had very high expectations about what it was going to be like being reunited, and I was very disappointed. I am still recovering from that right now.

This is what I tell my own half-sisters: "You don't know what it is like to be adopted and try to fit in to something like the family you have now. You guys have each other. There are all of you, and then there is me, by myself. You guys can huddle together and talk about me. I huddle with no one. I am not part of that because if I was, I would be able to be over there with you huddling and talking." They don't understand. It is just a feeling of not belonging anywhere—that I don't have the emotional support. Someone who would put me first before anything.

Joy Teran

JANET APPLEFORD *became pregnant at 19 while away from home at a small religious college. At first, Appleford kept her pregnancy a secret and planned to finish as much school as she could. She never told the birthfather. Prior to the birth of her son she wrote a letter to her parents outlining her situation and her plans to give her child up for adoption. Her family was supportive during her pregnancy, and offered to let her bring the child home. However, Appleford felt the taboos against single motherhood in the 1970s very strongly, and opted for adoption. Many years later Appleford was in a serious auto accident. Realizing that she might have died, Appleford searched for and found her only child when he was 14. Appleford, 42, is a health educator for Project ENABL (Education Now and Babies Later). Her son now lives with her.*

When I was pregnant, my parents would bring me home from the maternity home for visits. As we drove down the driveway, I would duck down in the back of the car so the neighbors wouldn't see me. When we got to the house I would go in and not leave until we went back to Los Angeles. One night somebody came to visit my parents, and I went to my room, closed the door, and didn't come out until they left. It was like we were all in a time warp. It's really bizarre that I would put up with that. I wasn't really ashamed during that time, but I felt I was doing what was right for my parents because it was their home.

I went home after the birth, and none of us knew what to do with my depression. I couldn't recognize it. When you are in the pits of depression you think that everybody is like that. After six weeks I went to work in a small hospital as a ward clerk. If you can imagine, part of my job was getting birth certificates signed. It was like the ultimate punishment. At that time in my life, the depression was bad. I was desperately afraid of going through the night. I hated the night. I tired to stay up all night because I was afraid I was going to die at night. At no point did I receive any counseling or therapy. Nothing was offered.

During that time, I started to have these feelings like I was glad that I didn't know where my son was because had I known, I would have gone and camped out on their doorstep. All I wanted was a glimpse of him. I just wanted to know if he was OK. I had fantasies about sitting in the doctor's office when all the mothers bring their babies in and that my son was one of them. I looked at people who didn't look alike to see if maybe some child was mine. That led to feelings that the adoption should never have happened. People said, "Just go home. It will take a while, but you will just forget about it and it will be fine. Just go on with your life. You'll have other kids, you'll get married, you'll have your work."

I entrenched myself in school after the adoption. I took twenty units at a time, and while doing that I worked at the hospital. I did anything I could not to think about it, not to give myself time. Almost immediately I started to question the adoption, but then I pushed it down so that I wouldn't have to feel. It was not until twelve years later that I finally admitted that trying to forget wasn't working. I was having real fits of depression during that year.

"Most people think that if they search for and find their child that the pain is going to be over. But after finding your child, you have to deal with the loss of the child."

Most people think that if they search for and find their child that the pain is going to be over. But after finding your child, you have to deal with the loss of the child. In the beginning I lost a baby. But when I found John, I lost a 1-year-old, a 2-year-old, and so on. On the first visit, the adoptive parents showed me the slides, and I watched my son grow from an infant into the adolescent I was sitting next to. I loved watching the slides, but it was like being slapped in the face with the fifteen years I had lost. It's not just the baby I lost, it was the whole thing.

It is difficult to understand my decision to relinquish my son. It actually feels more like a surrender than a relinquishment. I don't feel like there was a choice—single women didn't bring their babies home in 1970. My parents were supportive and loving towards me, but we never talked about the adoption. We were all trying to do what we thought was best. We didn't have any help in communicating. It wasn't until twelve years later that my father told me how angry he was at the adoption social worker, as he felt she was manipulative, unhelpful, and not looking out for me. But my father thought it was what I wanted—and I guess I thought it was what my parents wanted. We didn't know how to deal with or talk about the issue. I still don't understand how I could have given up my son.

During the fifteen years I did not have contact with my son, I always thought that if there had only been an abortion, I would not have the pain. It would have been gone. With adoption there was never any closure. People like to relate adoption and relinquishment to a death, but it's not the same. People go to a funeral when their children die. People who have children who die are encouraged to go and hold them and say good-bye. Birthmothers weren't. There is nothing. So you are constantly searching in your mind for this lost being, and that is one of the reasons why Concerned United Birthparents chose the logo of a bear and a cub. A mother bear who loses her child goes and looks for it and continues to look for it until she finds it.

Janet Appleford

REBECCA LEVERANT was adopted when she was a newborn. She accidentally found out

she was adopted when she was 23 years old from a woman who had been involved in the adoption. Her adoptive parents had not intended for her to know, hoping to spare her pain and feelings of rejection. Once her adoptive parents admitted to the adoption, they shared all the information they had about Leverant's birthparents. After six years, Leverant searched for and found her birthmother. Although the process has been tumultuous and painful, Leverant, 30, views it as an opportunity for growth. Leverant and her husband are co-directors of the Family Life Institute, an organization that facilitates all steps in the adoption process and provides support for all members of the adoption triangle.

When I was 23 years old I found out by mistake that I was adopted. My husband at the time was working in my brother's store, and a woman came in and said, "You are married to one of the Leverant daughters, the adopted one." My husband said, "Excuse me, I never heard that any of the daughters were adopted." The woman responded, "I am the secretary for the attorney that facilitated the adoption." Needless to say, at that point she began to feel like she had said something she wasn't supposed to because my husband looked so stunned. The woman then said, "Maybe I am mistaken."

My husband came home and told me what he'd heard at the store. I was shocked and called my parents, and they denied that I was adopted. At that point I knew, just by their reaction, that I had to be adopted. My sister, the biological child of our parents, was staying at my house, and I kept asking her, "Am I adopted?" She said, "I can't tell you. You have to hear it from Mom and Dad." She was just devastated because she had grown up knowing and had to live with this secret her whole life. An hour later my adoptive parents called back and said, "Yes, this is true. We are so sorry you found out this way. We never intended for you to know."

Finding out I was adopted was like having the rug pulled out from under me,

like the earth cracking. My sense of foundation was ruptured. It was a devastating experience to be told that all the things that I had formed my identity around were not true. I was in my early 20s and was starting to feel fairly solid about my sense of identity. On an unconscious level, I knew I was adopted. I blended with my family, but my body shape, talents, and intellectual development were very different.

There were spoken and unspoken reasons that my family didn't tell me. The spoken reason was to protect me from not feeling like a true member of the family, to protect me from criticism from peers and others, to protect me from the pain of knowing I was adopted and the subsequent feelings of rejection and abandonment. The unspoken reasons were their fears of what would happen when I found my birthmother. Would I want to leave?

My first reaction to finding out I was adopted was anger that my adoptive parents had withheld a piece of my identity. Your genetic identity is a profound part of who you are. I am still angry on some level, but after facilitating hundreds of adoptions as a licenced marriage, family, and child counselor, I have more understanding of why they didn't tell me. At the time they adopted me it wasn't as accepted as it is now. Finding out was traumatic, but my per-

sonality is such that I see the opportunity for growth in every event. Learning that I was adopted was an opportunity to grow up. Finding out also gave me permission to be an individual, and to know that my makeup is different from my adoptive family's. When I gained weight in college, I just assumed it was in the genes, and I tried to look like my mother and sister physically as a way of connecting. Finding out I was adopted allowed me to give up the expectation that I would be just like my family.

It took me six years to get to the point where I felt ready to search for my birthparents. Initially, I wanted to search, but I knew that if I had searched then, my motivation would've been wanting to get back at my adoptive parents. I needed to do some more work so that my motivation came from wanting to have truth, not from wanting to hurt somebody. I had a lot of anger at the hurt they had caused me. I was mad at my sister and brother, too. How could they not have told me? I was also mad at my birthparents. I didn't understand why they hadn't contacted me. It had been twenty-four years. It took me years to work through all that anger.

Once my adoptive parents admitted that I was adopted, they gave me all the information they had. The adoption was a private, closed adoption through an attorney and a doctor. There was no exchange of information. It was a fluke that I had my birthmother's name because my adoptive parents took the birth certificate from the hospital, and my birthmother had written her own name on it. The doctor that delivered me had died, and the attorney was bound by confidentiality. I found my birthmother by calling the operator and saying, "Give me all the listings for this name." The third number I reached was my grandfather. He is an attorney, and he was very inquisitive, almost interrogating me to make sure I was who I said I was. After ten minutes of talking to him, I guess he decided I was telling the truth, and he said, "Your mother will be very glad to hear from you. She's been actively searching for you for the past two years." He gave me my birthmother's phone number, and I called.

The reunion with my birthmother was an amazing experience. I will never forget it. There was an enormous sense of connection on the telephone. I asked, "How do you look? Tell me about the decision that you made. What did you go through? Where do you live? What do you do?" She is a psychologist, so we are in the same field. We have many emotional, intellectual, and physical attributes in common.

I talk with my adoptive parents about finding my birthmother. I communicate that I'm afraid of losing them, that I'm afraid they will feel like I have to choose. There are a lot of loyalty issues that come into play when you search, and it's difficult for those of us who have grown up in American society to deal with the sense of two families. If you come from other cultures in the world where there is more of a sense of extended family, I think it's more acceptable. In our society we have been programmed that our loyalty goes to our nuclear family. Everything in my being fights this sense of two families, and I feel like my loyalties are splitting. It creates a lot of fears, but luckily I am mature enough to be able to talk to my adoptive parents about unreal fears that I am going to be cut out of the family. They reassure me, but it is very difficult. It feels like if I get too close to my birthmother, that my adoptive parents will be hurt or think I don't love them as much. It's very difficult to integrate. I want my adoptive family and my biological family to be one family. The fact that they are separate is psychologically intolerable for me. My birthmother is coming out for a visit, and I am real excited about that because she is going to meet my adoptive family. I need to see them in the same room, sitting at the same table with me. My fantasy is that we will become one family.

I have not met my birthfather, but my birthmother has many positive things to say about him. Hearing those things alleviated my fears that she had been raped or that he was some derelict or drug addict. My birthparents were a couple in high school when my mother got pregnant. Evidently, my birthfather wanted to marry my birthmother and showed a lot of concern, but she ended the relationship. She didn't want to get married and went to another state to have me. For her, it's been a really hard struggle, and she has a tremendous sense of loss at not having raised me.

One of the struggles I went through when I found out I was adopted was deciding if I thought adoption was a good thing or a bad thing. What I have come to is that it is neither, that it is a condition, and it's a process you go through. It teaches us a lot about being human. It teaches us that just because we are physically able to have children doesn't mean we are always in the circumstances to raise them. We almost take our ability to procreate for granted, and adoption reminds us that there is a huge responsibility that goes along with it. I am a lover of possibilities, so I don't believe in any one way of doing adoptions. I can't say that I'm a propo-
nent of closed or open adoption, but I tend to think that some aspects of open adoption are more humane. The degree of openness varies so much today that I really do think it has to be personal. On a human level, I think it's important for people to know who they are, but if a birthmother doesn't want to give that information, it's important to respect her rights, too. I don't think any one human's rights are more valuable or more worthy than another's.

Adoption has a past, present, and future tradition. If you look at the story of Moses, it shows how adoption has an important role in developing the human aspects of people—compassion, love, and forgiveness. Moses' mother knew if she didn't pass him on, he would be killed. It must've been terrible to put him in a basket and send him down the river, not knowing where he would end up, which is the way it is for many birthmothers. To put the baby in the basket and send it down the river, Moses' mother must've had an element of tremendous faith that he would get somewhere safely and be taken care of. (The first questions my birthmother asked me were, "Was your family functional? Were you abused?") One part of the story I love is that Moses became a tremendous leader because it teaches us about the triumph of the human spirit over adversity, sacrifice, and sense of betrayal. I use that example because I feel a connection to it. It's valuable for people who survive all kinds of adversity and are stronger for it. Essentially, many of the issues faced by adopted people are human issues, but we have a concrete representation for them, so they are closer to the heart.

Rebecca Leverant

JERRY STADTMILLER was adopted at birth. When he was 21, he was shot in the face while serving in Vietnam. Subsequently, he underwent more than one hundred reconstructive operations. Stadtmiller began searching for his birthmother when he was 40, waiting until after the deaths of his adoptive parents in order to spare them and himself any turmoil his search may have created. He found out that his birthmother had died the day after his twelfth birthday, in 1959. Stadtmiller, 43, is married and has two children.

Growing up adopted I can say that I know the word "different," the expression "not a part of." Most people know who they are related to—I am floating. I have no beginnings. I felt envious and abandoned. Even if my adoptive parents had been able to have their own child, I think that child also would have felt abandoned by virtue of my adoptive parents' alcoholism. Yet, if there was ever any sense of rejection from aunts or uncles or cousins, whether it was intended or not, I would attribute it to the sense of this little piece of sand that created a pearl of a belief that I did not belong.

Growing up, there are always these medical forms to fill out. For most people it's probably just a pain in the ass filling out their history. For me, it was painful to write "not applicable," "adopted," "don't know." I had no family history. I was just out in space. On a spiritual level, it was almost as if either my soul or God said, "Jerry, you haven't gotten the message that we're all alike, so I'm going to make you look, as well as feel, different so you can learn how much alike we all are." I truly believe

that the least common denominator of man is pain. There are many, many flavors of pain. We isolate ourselves by virtue of our own hell. Yet, if we were to find points of commonality between my pain and yours, we'd say, "Oh, my God, we're in this together." I can't solve your problems, and you can't solve mine, but we can be here for each other in a supportive role.

When I was searching for my birthmother, my searcher called me up and said, "Jerry, this search is concluded. Your mother passed away on June 12, 1959." That happened to be the day after my twelfth birthday. Two months after receiving this news, my wife and I flew to Colma, California. It took us a long time to locate my birthmother's grave in a huge cemetery called Holy Cross. When we found her grave, I put a spray of flowers down, I knelt down, and I only got three words out before I completely collapsed. All I said was, "Gloria, it's Jerry." I just gushed with the feelings. I came away from that experience describing it as "other dimensional." I said to my birthmother that

"To be adopted is painful. Disregard any literature. Allow adoptees or birth-parents or adoptive parents to be the experts in discussing the issue."

I wished I could cure her cancer and bring her out of the grave. I asked her why she gave me up. I told her I felt I was a traveler and I'd come home to an empty house. I felt like I was looking through the back window and I saw a grave and I had waited too long to come home.

Before going to visit the grave, establishing a relationship with my birth-mother's younger sister, Arlene, was paramount in my mind. Once I visited Gloria's grave it became clear to me, "Gloria, you're the one I want the relationship with." It was like I wanted my arms to just penetrate the ground and lift her up and hug her. At that point I didn't know what my birthmother looked like, anything about the person she was, or her family relationships. I just knew she was the woman who carried me. She was the reason I was alive. I asked her questions like, "Did you know that I was shy? Did you know I got married? Do you know you have two beautiful granddaughters?" I talked to her about when she died, and I selfishly asked, "Gloria, were you thinking about me the day before you died?" I'll never give up my belief that the date of her death didn't have some relationship to my birthday. Afterward, I don't want to say I felt purged or cleansed, but I felt like a process had begun.

To be adopted is painful. Disregard any literature. Allow adoptees or birthparents or adoptive parents to be the experts in discussing the issue. Do not listen to the conventional wisdom because it's conventional misinformation. After I've shared my story with someone outside the adoption triangle, at least nine times out of ten I will receive the response, "Well, that's interesting." To which I want to say, "It goes way beyond interesting. I'm telling you about a secret pain that apparently you have no concept of." It's like two people speaking a different language.

At a Concerned United Birthparents [CUB] meeting last fall, I said adoption should be outlawed. I said to hell with opening records. Outlaw adoption. It is total bullshit that having an open adoption removes the pain. There's always going to be pain in adoption, and it is insanity to consider adoption without pain, open or closed.

Jerry Stadtmiller

DOROTHY BIEDEBACH

is a birthmother who was 20 years old when she became pregnant in 1960. She answered an ad in the newspaper for unwed expectant mothers to work in exchange for a place to live, then a common practice in New Zealand. Biedebach worked on a farm until her daughter, Ruth, was born. After giving her first child up for adoption, she moved to the United States, where she married and raised two more children. Biedebach was contacted by her birthdaughter and recently met her and her family when they came from New Zealand for a visit. Biedebach has married and divorced twice and is planning to move back to New Zealand.

Giving a child up for adoption really hasn't complicated my life, except for inconveniencing me for a few months. If I had kept my daughter, it would have been more complicated. After she was born I'm pretty sure I felt relief. Like I said, I wanted to get on with my life.

The adoption was something I sometimes thought about and sometimes didn't. It was just something that happened in my life, and periodically something would remind me of it. In fact, my sister's first child was born on the same day, two years later. So things like that would remind me. But to be quite honest, I didn't lose any sleep over the adoption. I had told my second daughter about Ruth and both my husbands knew. It wasn't that I completely put the adoption out of my mind, but I didn't try to hide it either.

Now that I have met Ruth, I kind of feel, well, not guilty, but I think, "Is there something wrong with me?" Because you see things on TV, people who reunite, and they are all crying, and I didn't do that. What good would that have done? That is all in the past. Nothing can change that. It is from today on. I got along with Ruth's kids wonderfully. I loved them. I loved Ruth's husband, but I found Ruth to be moody. We got along, but there were a couple of times when our voices were a little raised because I said what I thought. (It used to worry my father to death. He would say, "Dorothy, you don't have to say everything you think." But I do—that's the way I am.) I know that if I lived close to Ruth and her family that we would end up fighting.

Meeting them just felt like I was meeting friends that I haven't seen in a while. It was like I kind of knew them. Ever since they left, I have thought about it a lot, and I really am not sure how I feel, real deep down. I think so many things. I am glad that I know Ruth. I know that I want to keep in touch. I really don't think I could ever be as close to her as I am to my other two daughters. I thought about that, and I asked myself, "What is wrong with me?" Then I thought that Ruth is 32 years old. I really don't know that much about her. How much can you know about a person in two-and-a-half weeks?

I will see my birthdaughter and her family again, but if something happened and I didn't, I would just go on with my life. If I never, ever went back to New Zealand and never saw them again, it really wouldn't bother me. And that is what I keep thinking about— "Why do I feel like that?"

Dorothy Biedebach

DANIELLE MAREE BAKER *was adopted when she was 3 years old.*

She was conceived when her birthmother was raped (and beaten) by an employer. When Baker was born, her birthmother was told that the baby was stillborn. As a child, Baker was sexually and physically abused by her adoptive parents. She ran away from home when she was a teenager. Baker lived on the streets of New York and in foster homes until she was 20, when she married and joined a church. Baker's marriage ended, she miscarried, and she left the church. It took Baker, now 35, nine years to locate her birthmother and to piece together the story of her adoption. Baker says that she has always felt a strong connection with Marilyn Monroe, and was later told by her birthmother that she is related to Monroe.

I grew up believing that nobody wanted me—this is what I was told by my adoptive parents. They told me, "Nobody else wanted you. You were in a series of foster homes and were a problem child. We came along and wanted to do our Christian duty. You were so sickly and pathetic, and we were willing to take you in when everyone else had failed with you." I thoroughly believed this all my life, until four years ago.

My adoptive mother was cold and cruel to me from the very beginning. She would tie me to the kitchen table with bootstraps to give me enemas. She was always hostile toward me, and I felt that she never liked me. My father, on the other hand, adored me—when I was little. I was his angel from God. I think it was his idea to adopt me. When my sister was adopted, my adoptive father "fired" me. She was his new bundle of joy. My sister was another "gotten child." Adoptees don't get born, they get "gotten". I felt procured like furniture, like a commodity.

I think adoption as we know it should stop. This is a radical statement, but it doesn't feel radical to me, as something of an "expert" on adoption. I am very involved in adoption issues, and go to conferences and give presentations. My idea of adoption would be to provide homes to needy children rather than supplying children to needy homes.

Perhaps in the future I would be willing to open my home to a child and be a guardian, but I would not try to pretend I was a mother or that I had given birth to the child. I would not hide a child's heritage or medical history or withhold its civil rights and keep it oppressed. I would not manipulate the truth. What I am suggesting is more like foster care. I would take a child in, but I wouldn't get the pink slip. I wouldn't own that child; that child owns himself. I would be helping out. I would be a substitute caregiver and not hold myself out as a parent. I would be called Danielle, not Mommy or Auntie.

If people want to take a child who isn't theirs into their home, that's fine, but that doesn't necessarily make them wonderful people, they are not heroes. They want to adopt because they want to have a child; they are getting just what they want. If you take a child in, you should walk into it knowing what you are getting involved in. The child might not be with you permanently. It's just like marriage; you have to accept that there is divorce. It exists. It might happen to you even though you are perfectly content. The child might not be happy and want to leave. There has to be some kind of divorce built into the adoption system.

I tried to get unadopted—it doesn't happen. I tried everything. We finally went

"This is my story, and most people would not trade with me. But it is mine, it is the truth, and it has been kept from me my whole life. People out there have had the truth about me and I didn't have the same information. You have to be an adoptee to hear how absurd that is."

to court, and I was disinherited legally at 16. I tried to say, "This adoption isn't working out. What are my recourses?" The next option should have been to contact my birthmother and see if she wanted me to come home. Instead, I was put into foster homes when I was 16 years old and further abused. My birthmother now tells me she would have gladly taken me if somebody had called her.

When someone says, "I am desperate to have a child," people say, "That's normal." When you say, "I am desperate to have a relationship," they send you to a therapist. There is something wrong. I would ask, "Why are you desperate to have a child?" I can see we are driven to procreate, but to get a child from someone else is not procreation. It's something else altogether that needs to be looked at. Therapy has to be part of the deal. Adoption is an ineffective cure for infertility. I am now infertile, and I feel that I can really address this issue. A lot of times when people adopt they are trying to plug up a hole. They are not seeing the child as human with needs and wants and feelings and a history and rights. Their desperation drives them to fill the void. The pathology needs to be worked through before guardianship can be considered.

This is my story, and most people would not trade with me. But it is mine, it is the truth, and it has been kept from me my whole life. People out there have had the truth about me and I didn't have the same information. You have to be an adoptee to hear how absurd that is. Not only do I not know about me, but someone else does. That makes me crazy.

I now have a wonderul, ongoing relationship with my birthmother of four years duration. Our relationship is full of ups and downs, but it is extremely healing and fulfilling. This relationship has allowed me to actually go back to the womb and start over in fast forward. However, it doesn't erase the primal wound.

Danielle Maree Baker

DAVIS DENTON

was adopted at birth. He and his adopted sister began searching for their respective birthmothers when they were in their early 20s. They found them five years later, within a week of each other. Denton later met his birthfather. As a result of finding his birthparents, Denton, 29, became much closer to his adoptive parents and sister.

I went through a lot looking for my birthmother because I didn't know who I was going to meet. My goal was not to ruin somebody's life or to be intrusive. I felt strongly about that. All I wanted to do was to offer an invitation. If my birthmother declined, that would be that. But I did want to see her and still respect her rights. I wanted to do it in a way that I could tell her I had done everything I could to get to see her. I thought about a phone call and decided against it because number one, you don't know who might be listening on the line, and, number two, if she hung up, I would never call back. It would be a shocking phone call to get. I thought about sending a letter, and I didn't want to do that for the same reasons. I didn't know who might read the letter, and I wanted to be absolutely certain my birthmother received it. I decided when I flew home for Christmas that I would drive up to the city where my birthmother lived and hand-deliver a letter to her.

My adoptive parents were real nice. They asked if I wanted them to come with me, which really moved me because they disapproved of the search. If it were up to them, they would never do it. They are sociologists and to them, the nature-nurture battle is 99.9 percent nurture, yet my adoptive parents love me and feel that if something is important to me they will support it. I told them, "Thanks, but this is one of those things I have to do for myself. It would be like having someone propose marriage for you."

I drove up and found the address right away and was just hanging out in my car. It was a rainy day, and I was waiting across the parking lot of my birthmother's condo complex. I was trying to be inconspicuous, but it was raining, and so every now and then I had to have the windshield wipers on so I could see who was there. I felt really conspicuous being there. Emotionally, I was on a roller coaster. I had been up late the night before writing the letter. I tried to write it on the plane and started crying and feared I was going to have a nervous breakdown.

A car came that looked like it was going to my birthmother's condo. Sure enough, it did. Three people got out. It was a little bit blurry, and I couldn't see anything well. Twenty-five minutes later they all came out again and hopped in the car and left. I was saying to myself, "OK, I'll follow them." I was being cool. I have watched the cop shows, and I know you don't get right behind someone you're following, so I was slow coming out of the parking lot. Just as I was pulling out, someone began doing a twelve-point turn, and they were right in my way. I thought, "Move! I can't believe you're in front of me." By the time this person did their parking maneuver, the car was long gone. By that point I was a nervous wreck, and I was in no condition to meet anybody, much less my birthmother. So I went and got a hotel room, got a meal, and just relaxed. I thought that at the worst, I had come up here and it wasn't going to work out. I might have to try it another time, and it's only a one-day drive. I got to

"There needs to be some acknowledgement that being adopted is a different way of growing up, with its own issues and risks."

the point where I calmed myself and got something to eat, and I went back to stake things out again and tried to remain calm.

About an hour after I returned, my birthmother drove off again and I followed—much closer this time. She pulled into a shopping center to go to a grocery store, but in the parking lot, I became a little confused. I was not exactly sure which was her car. I chose the one I thought was hers and parked across from it, where I could see. All I could think of at the time was the serenity prayer. I got stuck on the part that says, "...the courage to do the things you can do." I told myself, "I can walk over and hand somebody a letter. I can do it. All I have to do is walk over there." So, after one false alarm (a woman going to the next car), my birthmother walked out, and I just went up and asked her name. She wanted to know why, and I said that I had a personal and confidential letter for her eyes only. I handed it to her, and then I left. I went back to my hotel room and waited. Essentially in the letter I told her who I was, my birth date, and that it was a special day for me and I thought for her too. If it was, I wanted to assure her that I was not trying to invade her privacy or to look for a surrogate family or anything like that. I was just trying to get a better sense of who I am and at some point maybe have a chance to meet her. I gave the phone number and extension of the hotel room that I was going to be at that night. I also gave my home phone so she could call me any time. I couldn't bring myself to say, "If and when at any point you feel like you want to contact me, then please do so." The letter also contained a few things— a poem, a few pictures, and a brief outline of my life, which I hoped would whet her appetite for more.

In my hotel room I began pacing. I wanted to call my sister and say, "Oh, it failed. It didn't go well at all." I thought, "Well, who knows, maybe she'll call." So I stayed off the phone and paced, and in just a few minutes I heard a knock at the door. I opened the door, and there was my birthmother. She said, "That was a lovely letter," and she came in and gave me a hug. Although I thought I was ready for every eventuality, this was the one I didn't allow myself to think about. I didn't know what to do. Most of the reunions I had read about happened in public places, so everyone felt a little safer. I was very conscious of that, yet she just said, "You know, I didn't even get a chance to finish the letter. It would be fine if we want to talk here, but I am just a little thirsty because I am excited." And I said, "I will go get you a drink, and you can finish the letter." I was floating downstairs. I was just beaming, and the girls at the desk were smiling back. I know that they didn't know the significance of it, but it was good to have the acknowledgement.

As we talked, I was struck by her warm personality. I read a fair amount about reunions, and some had written that it is like falling in love. That was the strongest feeling that I can remember. It was just like falling in love. Months later, I was still adjusting to this whole thing. Adjusting to how our family was dealing with it. Initially, it was hard on my adoptive parents. It didn't occur to any of us that it would work out this well. My adoptive parents were fearful that it was going to work out badly. But some of their own fears were about it working out well. They feared everything was going to fall apart, but it didn't. I tried to give them a lot of reassurance. My sister and I were celebrating, it was so wonderful. Our adoptive parents were glad for us, but it wasn't a celebration. Meeting my birthparents changed my relationship with my adoptive parents. We can relate to each other as adults, with frailties and strong points. It brought us closer as a family, and we could talk about all this stuff that didn't get talked about much as we were growing up.

People can't pretend that a birthmother will carry a baby to term, give it up, and then go on with her life as if nothing happened. Or that an infertile couple will easily give up their desire for a biological family and deny any difference between an adopted and a biological child. There needs to be some acknowledgement that being adopted is a different way of growing up, with its own issues and risks. It is a unique way. The main thing I key on is that it is a loss. That everybody at some time suffers a loss, and if it goes unacknowledged, then it is not healthy.

I was able to locate my birthfather about a year after meeting my birthmother. This is a poem he wrote to me just after we met. It says, "To Davis. Of course each life's a journey. Each of us could prepare a map in retrospect, from stories, lies, and memories, tracing backwards, arrival to origin. Who could know in advance the contours of the horizon, the features of the chart? Who could know where lies the channel to the heart?"

Davis Denton

BARBARA DUDREAR

gave a child up for adoption when she was 21. Two years later she had a second child, who died shortly after birth. When her birthdaughter was 26, Dudrear contacted her, and after four years of sometimes angry correspondence, they met. Dudrear, 53, is now divorced and has no other children. The cat in the photograph is a recent gift from her daughter.

I wasn't pregnant because that's what I wanted to be. It was because of my irresponsibility, my willingness not to be responsible for my sexuality that allowed me to put total trust in the male. It was partly due to the times in which I was raised, in the 1940s and 1950s. At that time I viewed myself according to how the male viewed me. How attractive I was had a great deal to do with my sexuality. I didn't know about containing myself. It was a betrayal of myself too, to give myself away so easily. I didn't consider myself as creating a child. I considered myself to be having a good time, feeling wanted, giving love, receiving love—that's what sex was. I had no intention of having children. I regret my irresponsibility and ignorance about contraceptives.

When I told my mother and father that I was pregnant, it was very shocking for them. I was a child they had put their hopes on, the one who would go to college. Those hopes were dashed. I think they were put in a position that must be very hard for parents—to be someplace where they don't know what to do. Their response was not to recognize me as a daughter they had loved for 21 years, who was part of the family, and to whom they had a commitment to care for. My mother could only call me a whore. That's all she could say. My father sat and cried, and then, when he could speak, he asked me to leave, saying, "This is my neighborhood." Gosh knows where this shame comes from, but it overwhelms us and separates us

from our parents, and parents from their bonds with their children.

I also felt ashamed. I, too, am part of my culture, accepting the belief system without thought. I had judged two of my friends in high school who got pregnant—I judged them harshly, unkindly, and thoughtlessly. It was a reaction, not a response. The thinking at the time was, "There's a rule, you break it, and here's the penalty." It doesn't come from a place really deep inside a person. A rule has been broken, and that becomes the important part—the rule, rather than the human who broke the rule. It was very devastating for me to be betrayed by the two people I had grown up with. It threw me into the circumstance of not ever knowing my parents and shifted my ground, my center of being. When my pregnancy started being known, I then bore the humiliation and was scapegoated in my family. They couldn't tell me that they were disappointed and how it hurt. They weren't able to express their feelings, but what they could do was put me away. We also do that with people who are dying. We put them away. We don't want to watch their pain.

I wrote to the birthfather's family. They lived in Kansas, and I had the address and the mother's name. I wrote to the mother, so it would be a woman-to-woman kind of thing. I wasn't asking for money, I was asking for emotional support. When the self-respect leaves, the shame and humiliation take over. Then there is the physical vulnerability

of being pregnant. I couldn't accept that someone around me would not help me. I went from door to door looking for a place to stay. I got a letter back from the mother's attorney stating that my boyfriend had always been a bad boy, that he caused his mother lots of trouble, and that he had gotten another girl pregnant. I was told not to contact her again, and not to look to her for any kind of help.

I wondered if these people realized that it wasn't just me they were ignoring, but another life, their grandchild. It began to seem that I was the only one aware of this life. Yet when anybody else in the family was married and pregnant—a cousin, an aunt, my older sister—it was a joy, and they spread the news. Because I wasn't married and I had sex out of wedlock, the door was really closed. There was no way to get in that door. I was a whore. Is this a whore's act? What was so wrong with me that my father wanted me out of the neighborhood?

My doctor mentioned adoption as a possibility. He knew a doctor's family where there was infertility and thought they'd be good parents. Adoption seemed like the only thing I could do because of the social pressure from those who knew I was pregnant. The attitude was, "A good mother would give her child up. A good mother would keep her child from being called a bastard. A good daughter would not bring shame to the family with a child bearing her surname." All of these were attitudes I might have expressed at one time, too. Only now do I realize how cruel and really how stupid they are. I was vulnerable, and I didn't know how to withstand the pressure of my culture. I was too frightened to be outside of my belief system because

that's the unknown.

I always thought about my daughter. When I returned to college I got a teaching degree, and my first year of teaching was with fifth-graders. That's the grade my daughter would have been in at the time. The next year she was in sixth grade, and I taught sixth grade. I set it up so every year I taught children who would be her age. I wanted to be around people who would be my daughter's age. It wasn't a penance in that I was making up for her. It was a contribution to children's lives. All the teaching I did was with the economically disadvantaged, which was what I was when I was pregnant. Had I had the funds, I could have kept my daughter, or I could have gotten an abortion.

The scenario in my mind told me that when my daughter finished college she would want to find me. I waited for her, and she didn't come. One morning I woke up, and something had changed within me. I began to worry about her well-being. It then occurred to me to search. So I returned to San Diego, realizing that this was where my pathology was to be confronted. In preparing to search, I went back through all my experiences, back to the place of conception, to where the birthfather was told, to the hospital. I was starting to plumb the depths of what was there, and it brought forward a grief that was frightening to me.

With the grief came the horror of having relinquished a daughter, the horror of having given her to strangers. How could I do that? How? Even in an open adoption they would still be strangers! I gave her to strangers. I was reading adoption literature, and I became aware of the dark side of adoption. It was then that I allowed myself to realize the full horror of giving a child away, and I paced the floor all night long. It was my way of getting through. It wasn't anything I could sleep through. I faced the horror, and with it came the grief. In order to survive I learned to be cunning with myself. I learned that there was a way to work with death to keep myself alive. At the end of every six-month period I allowed myself the opportunity to kill myself if I chose to. Every six months I could renew my contract with life. So I always had those hours before renewing my contract with life, where I had permission to die. This is how I stayed alive, for three, four years, when my search was going on and I had first contacted my daughter. Giving myself permission to die helped me stay alive.

I contacted my daughter by letter. Two weeks later, she wrote to me and called me her "alleged" biological mother. She questioned the whereabouts of her birthfather and said that in a million years she could never give up a child. She was angry. I was surprised by it. We kept writing, but each time I had no idea if there would be further communication. She expected to find the person she had been told about. When she was 6, her adoptive grandmother told her that the reason she had birthmarks was because her birthmother wore a girdle that had crushed her head. It must have been horrifying to hear that your mother would crush your head. My daughter was also told that she would have gone to an orphanage, if they hadn't taken her. When I contacted my daughter I threw her life into chaos. The letters went back and forth. I sent the medical documents showing that forceps had been used, and she was willing to say, "Yes, that's more reasonable. I know my grandmother didn't mean to harm me. She only

meant to make sure that I loved my adoptive family." Unfortunately, that's one of the things that often happens. We cripple our children, believing they will love us for it, never recognizing how wrong it is.

My daughter and I are new in our relationship. I like her a lot. She doesn't look like me. I didn't find someone I recognized as a younger me. She looks like her father, at times she looks like my mother, which makes me happy. She's familiar, but I can't quite place her yet. It's an odd feeling. I don't know when that will change, probably when we spend more time together.

The Western world is not kind to the unwed, and it's especially unkind to the unwed who are pregnant. It's also unkind to those who are called barren or sterile. It seems to me that something is wrong in our thinking. There are stigmas in both directions, and the children get caught right in the middle. If I could write the laws, adoptive parents would be legal guardians rather than legal parents, so that the child would not be severed from the birth family. Frankly, I don't see how open adoption can work, especially when the adoption can close whenever the adoptive parents choose.

I guess I'm back to the issue of responsibility. I need to be responsible for the life I create. For myself, I would prefer to be responsible for an abortion rather than an adoption, since adoption puts a child at psychological risk, and that's hard for a mother to live with. The most responsible option, of course, would be for me to have kept my child.

Barbara Dudrear

JAY KAQUATOSH'S birthmother and birthfather lived on an Indian reservation in Wisconsin. When Kaquatosh's mother was pregnant with him, his father took their three sons and left, claiming he was uncertain that he had fathered Kaquatosh. As an infant, Kaquatosh contracted pneumonia, and his maternal uncle took Kaquatosh home with him because his mother was considered to be an alcoholic and unable to provide adequate care for her son. Kaquatosh was eventually adopted by his uncle. The family continued to visit his birthmother periodically at the reservation. When Kaquatosh was 11, one of his half-brothers by his birthmother told him he was adopted and that his aunt was really his birthmother.

When I was 11, I found out I was adopted. I didn't say anything. I didn't say to my real mother, "I know." I just locked it up and went on. It was traumatizing. Between the time when I was 11 until I was 15, something in me changed, and a lot of times I just didn't care at all. I was really a mixed-up kid. I hated my adoptive parents. I'd just tell them, "Fuck off, I don't want you to love me." That would be my way of getting back at them. I really regret it now. My adoptive dad drank a lot, really heavily, and he used to hit me forcefully. To get away from it all, I'd go out and break laws just to get away. A couple of times I went out and broke a guy's window or stole something out of a car so I'd get thrown in jail and be safe. I'd have some place to stay where nobody was yelling at me or hitting me. I thought, " I don't have to go to school, jail is really cool." I should have been scared out of my wits in jail, but I wasn't. I felt safe.

Finally, I got sent away to a juvenile facility for two years. I did a lot of changing there. There was a class at the facility called Indian Tribes of Wisconsin that was about American Indian culture. Before, on the reservation, I saw slums. I saw beer bottles smashed all over the roads, drunk people walking the streets. Basically that's what I thought about Indians. When I was young, I had no sense of who I was. That class on Indian tribes taught me a lot about my heritage and changed my view of who I was. After being there, I learned to forgive—I forgave a lot. I didn't forget—it's always there—I just handle it in different ways. I'm never going to go back that way again. I'm never going to hit that road where I'm doing all these wrong things and hurting people—hurting myself, mostly.

When I met my birthfather, it was just something that hit me inside. I didn't want to kill my birthfather, but I often thought, "I'm going to beat the shit out of him if I see him. If I ever see my real dad, I'm just going to beat him for turning his back on me and my mother when she was pregnant." Sometimes, I thought that. After talking to him, he said that he didn't know I was his for sure and that's what everyone else told me, so I figured maybe that's what it was.

It was a shock to find out I had three real, full brothers. I got to meet one of them. When I saw him, I knew for sure that his father was my real dad. This guy was to a T my twin brother. He was just a little bit heavier, but he had the same mustache, same hair, same height. It was me, I was looking at me. My brother just stared at me—-whew! I saw my dad and my brother for about an hour, and that was it. I left them, and I haven't seen them since.

Jay Kaquatosh

PATTI FIFE is a birthmother who was 21 years old when she and her husband separated. Fife was living alone with her 2-year-old son, Jed, when she became pregnant with her second child, Kendall. The father of the baby wanted to marry Fife, but she refused. Fife gave Kendall up for adoption because she felt it would have been impossible as a single parent to care for a newborn and a 2-year-old in addition to finishing college. Fife later remarried and had another child, Bryhannah, in 1987.

Abortion is OK for some people, but it's not OK for me. If I hadn't had my son, Jed, I probably would have had an abortion when I got pregnant with Kendall. But when I had a child, I knew that thing moving around inside of me was actually a little person. For me, abortion was not an alternative. I felt good about giving Kendall up for adoption because she would add a lot to somebody's life. Whereas, if I had had an abortion, she would have just been something else sucked into a jar. I had to explain to people who knew I was pregnant where this baby went. I was called names worse than a murderess. I was told really nasty things. People don't give their children away. You give away puppies, and you give away kittens, but you don't give away your children. It's OK to have an abortion, that's fine with these people, but you don't give birth to a child and give it away. My girlfriend and I were talking in the supermarket, and this man that I didn't know from Adam came up and started telling me what a terrible person I was. He asked how I could just give my child away, like it was just some common dog. I was totally floored, I had to leave the grocery store. I have lost some friends over the adoption, and it took a long, long time before some of them could even talk about it and hear my side of why I did what I did.

When I was pregnant, I called a place called Lifeline in Lancaster, California, where I was living at the time. They told me about lawyers that handle adoptions, and I contacted the lawyer

that handled our adoption. I spoke to him and his secretary and arranged to see the files on some couples, including the couple that adopted my daughter. By the time I picked out the adoptive parents for my baby, I was close to eight months pregnant. I met the adoptive couple about two weeks later. We had lunch, and I didn't see them again until after the baby was born. We went through a private attorney. I didn't want to give my baby to the county, because I felt once the baby was sucked into the county system, they're gone. I didn't want that. At least I wanted to know where my baby was, and I wanted to meet the people who were going to raise my baby. Also, the not knowing is the hardest part. If you can look these people dead in the eye, you can tell a lot about people with just your gut feelings. Whereas with the county it's just the next person in line.

In the hospital, nobody would talk to me about adoption. It was taboo. They put me in a room that contained folding chairs and a bed down at the end of a corridor. I had to demand my baby. I was furious. I told them point blank, "I have signed no paperwork giving up custody, and until I do, you people are not to keep my baby from me." The hospital had had a disastrous experience with a cooperative adoption and absolutely refused to let the adoptive parents near me or the baby until I left the hospital. The doctor never said a word. Not a word. We did have a very brief discussion when I told him I was placing the baby for adoption. He said,

"OK, I just want to let you know that the baby seems pretty healthy, and everything looks fine in your pregnancy." And that was the whole discussion.

When I walked out of the hospital, I was numb. Everything had happened so quickly. I was pregnant, I went into labor, I had a baby, I went home. I was supposed to take a little baby home, and I didn't, so part of my mind just totally blocked it out. It was too painful, I couldn't deal with it. I told myself, "I will just put it away until I can." Kendall was born Friday morning, and I was back in school Monday. It was like my life did not change; there wasn't even a glitch, other than the two days I was in the hospital.

Later, I became angry with myself for not being able to provide a better, more stable home for my daughter. If I didn't have my son, I would have kept Kendall. There would have been no question about it. But I knew how difficult it was. I knew I couldn't finish school and raise a 2-year-old child and a newborn. It would have been impossible as a single parent.

When the adoption was over it was a relief. Initially, we had set up progress reports every six months where I'd get a letter and a picture or something to let me know that the baby was OK. That's basically how it went until Kendall was 2. That was the only time that I ever called Kendall and made the initial contact. It was her birthday, and I wanted to see her. It was the first time that I ever really, really wanted to see her. I called the lawyer and left the phone number where I was. The lawyer called the family, and the adoptive mother called me back. She said the only cruel thing that she has ever said to me. She said, "Well, sometimes we just want to forget that she's adopted, and we don't want you to see her right now." I dropped the phone. It made me feel like all the talk that had gone on about progress reports and things of that nature was totally false. I was really depressed. At that time the door swung wide open, and everything that had been bottled up fell out. It was very, very difficult. With the holidays and Kendall's birthday, I was in a deep depression. I didn't want to talk to anybody. I didn't want to see anybody. The only person that I wanted any contact with was my son.

Now my relationship with Kendall is more like that of an aunt or sister. I try really hard not to do parenting. I don't discipline her unless she's in my house. I have disciplined her one time in my house in front of her adoptive parents, and then I just walked around on eggshells because I didn't know whether they'd take Kendall home and say, "You did that, and we don't like it, and you can't ever see her again." So I walk real carefully around issues like that. If Kendall asks me something, I say, "You have to ask your mom and dad. If they say it's OK, it's OK by me." I have become good friends with Kendall's adoptive mother. We talk about if Kendall decides that she does not wish to continue our relationship, then the adoptive mother and I will continue it because we are friends. The adoptive mother is the kind of person that if I were to meet her outside of this situation, I would still like her and still want to be her friend. It's not like I'm just her friend because she's raising Kendall, we go way past that. The adoptive mother is a psychologist, which is pretty nice because there are a lot of times that I'll be really confused, and I'll call her on the phone and say, "What's going on here? I need a little counseling on the phone." But it took about five years before I could say it.

When my son, Jed, was about 6, we started seeing the adoptive parents again. Jed was just terrified. He would do something, and I would say, "Jed, please don't do that," and he'd burst into tears and fall apart. I was wondering what was going on, and I finally learned that Jed was afraid that unless he was absolutely perfect, I was going to give him away. Kids are not perfect at 6—nobody's perfect at any age. It took a long time for Jed to feel comfortable. He tried so hard for so long because he didn't want me to give him away. I never said to Jed that I was going to give him away. As for Bryhannah, she's now 4 and getting to where she can understand at the very outside fringes what's going on.

My parents live about a mile away from here. They are just now starting to feel comfortable with Kendall. For a long time they were afraid to even start a relationship, other than an extremely superficial one, with her for fear that the adoptive parents would take her away. It's a very, very difficult thing because you have so many people's needs and emotions that you have to consider. You can't just say, "Well, I'm going to do this because it is best for me." You have to look at it and ask, "Is it best for Kendall? Is it best for the adoptive parents? Is it best for Patti? Is it best for all the kids, or for all the adults?" And it's not always best for everybody, but I have to go with the flow. If you can't sit down and say what's best, then it's not going to work.

In my opinion, cooperative adoptions are by far the best kind. I know Kendall is never going to look at herself in the mirror and say, "Who do I look like? Do I have brothers and sisters? Do I have any aunts, uncles, grandparents?" She's never going to have to do that. If a medical emergency arises down the road, she's going to pick up the phone and say, "Hey, Patti, does this run in our family?"

Patti Fife

BARBARA SHAW

became pregnant when she was 22. Shaw has no memory of the first and only time she slept with the birthfather, a medical student who she had dated for about three weeks. She lived in a maternity home for about five months and relinquished her son at birth. After learning about Concerned United Birthparents, Shaw, 45, searched for and found her son, but he has been unwilling to contact her.

The maternity home had a very warm atmosphere, and they took care of us physically—good meals, vitamins, that sort of thing. I was the oldest, at 22. There was one 13-year-old girl, which was very sad. One of the hardest things at the maternity home was that our identity was immediately taken from us. On all our mail there was a black marker covering up our last names and all the return addresses. When we were taken out to the stores, we had to wear coats, and then after a certain point, we weren't allowed to leave the home. The last couple months of my pregnancy my outside world was shut in by a tall wooden fence in the backyard. It was a residential neighborhood, and the fence prevented anyone from seeing us. There were no parenting classes and no counseling because we were not considered mothers, only bodies carrying children for other people. A man came to discuss birth control. The thing that stands out in my mind is what he said about not getting pregnant: "Well, just wear a tight girdle." And he laughed.

After my son was delivered, I was kept separate from the maternity ward so that no one would know I was an unwed mother. I was luckier than some of my birthmother friends who were never allowed to see their babies. The hospital allowed me to have my son for three days. He was really beautiful, and I remember wondering if he would grow up to be a football player. My caseworker told my mother she would never be his grandmother.

I went back to the home after the delivery, and my caseworker came to see me to sign the relinquishment papers. The caseworker shoved the papers at me, but I refused to sign. I was slumped down in my chair with my arms crossed feeling very defiant. We'd been in there for about thirty minutes, and she was very angry. She said, "You are the most selfish person I ever met. If you loved this child you would sign these papers." I'll never get over the fact that I believed it. She told me I would never see my son again. Afterwards, I went up to my room and cried. One of the staff came in and said, "Now, dry your eyes. You'll have more children. Get on with your life." I didn't understand why I was being punished for being single. But I stopped crying and until recently have not cried since. Those first few months I spent most of my nights after work wandering around the local shopping center, looking for babies and going into baby stores.

One day in 1984, I opened up the Sunday newspaper, and there was an article on Concerned United Birthparents [CUB]. I'll never forget the feeling of sitting there thinking, "What! What do you mean there are women searching?" I was astonished that I could be allowed to search. I wrote for information and started opening up. On a hike with two friends, I told them about my son. That was a big step for me because it was something I just never talked about. I was starting to come out of the closet.

"When you hold something in for so long, it's an incredible feeling when you are finally able to share it....I've gone from twenty years of silence to being very verbal."

When I first moved to California, I worked for a newspaper. One day I opened the paper and there was an article on the San Diego chapter of CUB, which was having a table at the Adoption Forum. I will never forget the emotions I had when I walked up to the CUB table. I walked back and forth for a while because I thought that as soon as I go up to the table, people would know I'm a birthmother. Finally I went over, and everyone was very nice, asking, "Can I help you?" I said, "Oh no, not really." And then I asked, "So what exactly do you do?" And they told me.

About two months later, I went to my first CUB meeting. I was terrified because it was so emotional. At first I thought, "What am I doing here?" When you hold something in for so long, it's an incredible feeling when you are finally able to share it. Here were other women who felt just as I did. I was so overwhelmed, I couldn't go back to another meeting for months. But I did eventually go back, and it was as if the floodgates had been opened. Since then, I've gone from twenty years of silence to being very verbal, much to the discomfort of family and friends. I even wrote a newspaper column about being a birthmother.

My son was found within ten days of my beginning the search. I was absolutely elated. I felt like I had been shot to the stars—literally floating on air. I was ecstatic. It was incredible just to have a name for my son, and then to receive pictures. I didn't know where he was living at the time, so every time I went out, I would embarrass myself by staring at every group of young guys I saw.

Eventually, I went back to school and completed my master's degree, and from all outward appearances, I've had a pretty exciting life—traveling, living in London, Colorado, San Diego. I know some of my married friends have envied my carefree life-style. Underneath all that was twenty years of fighting off depression, and a constant restlessness I couldn't understand. I took no pleasure in other people's children and found it difficult to hold babies.

One of the things I'm gaining from finding my lost son is the opportunity to grieve for the lost years. I was told by his family that he has no interest or need to get to know me. But even if he did, I would still have to grieve. I cry nearly every day. And because I feel so much joy too, it's like a roller coaster. One of the things I've found most amazing through this whole process is how people, especially women, would understand losing a child, but they don't. Older people should know better, but maybe the younger ones think that relinquishment was voluntary back then, but it wasn't. Nobody put a gun to our heads, but society sort of did. People are very puzzled. They really don't understand why we think of this as a loss.

Barbara Shaw

ALEX THOMPSON

was adopted when he was two months old. His birthparents were college students and involved in an interracial relationship. Thompson was adopted into a Caucasian family. He became aware that he was adopted when he was about 6 years old. When Thompson was 18, he decided to search for his birthparents. To date, he has not found them.

I found out I was adopted when I was old enough to understand what it meant. My adoptive family is Caucasian, so I realized there was a difference in the color of our skin. I was about 13 when I started thinking about meeting my birthparents. My brother and I got into a lot of trouble for stealing. When my adoptive parents punished us, I'd have these fits where I wanted to find out who my birthmother was. "My real mom wouldn't do this kind of stuff to me," I'd think. That's when I first started admitting that I wanted to know who she was. Later I realized that I just wanted to know.

When I was 17 I started talking to other people about being adopted and about finding their birthparents. I saw an ad in the paper for a detective who can track down anyone, but it turned out to be very expensive. He gave me the name of a children's services organization, and I got some information from them. I'm positive I want to find my birthparents. I didn't really do anything about searching for my birthparents when I was younger because of my adoptive mom's reaction. She was kind of upset. Maybe she thought she wasn't a good enough parent or something. When I talked to her about it, I could see her getting teary-eyed, and I told her I wish she could be in my shoes. I reassured her that she was a fine parent and it was just my curiosity. My adoptive dad said, "What does it matter? Why do you need to find your birthparents?"

I know that I was born in Panorama City in Los Angeles. Either my birthfather was black and my birthmother was white or the other way around, I'm not sure. I think my adoptive parents met them. They were in their teens and couldn't afford to have a kid, so I was put up for adoption. I grew up black in an all-white school. In school we did family trees, and I found the symbol for my family's last name, Thompson. But it wasn't really my blood, and I wanted to know what my very own family's last name was.

I don't have a specific fantasy about my birthparents. Chances are they were teenagers and don't even know each other now. The hardest thing about being adopted is curiosity about my birthparents. I have a natural curiosity inside of me. Sometimes I go into a market or I'm in a crowd of people, and I just wonder if someone in that crowd is related to me in some way. It's hard not knowing. I feel like a puzzle with one piece missing. I would like to get a glimpse of my natural parents walking down the street. If I could talk to them, that would be great. I would like them to give me more of an explanation. I would like to know my last name, find out where I came from, know where I originated.

Alex Thompson

MARY MEDLIN is a birthmother who became pregnant when she was a 20-year-old college student. The birthfather, also a college student, is the son of close friends of her family. After giving her daughter up for adoption, Medlin later married and had a second child, Timothy, eleven years after having her daughter. Subsequent to Timothy's birth, Medlin searched for and found her daughter, who was 11 years old at the time. To date, Medlin has not met her daughter because her daughter and her daughter's adoptive parents have chosen not to meet with her. Medlin, 43, feels she has paid a heavy emotional price for giving up her child for adoption.*

I was so taken aback by the birthfather's response when he found out I was pregnant. He just didn't want to be involved and pretty much said, "It is your problem." When I went home, the big issue with my father was the fact that I wasn't a virgin anymore, rather than I was going to have a child and how we were going to deal with this. The overriding issue for my parents at the time, which seems so strange now, was that nobody find out. So I went to a Catholic home for unwed mothers near Washington, D.C., where I stayed for five months.

At first, I alternated between being terrified of being pregnant and just hoping it would somehow miraculously go away. Once I got there, I didn't mind the place, probably because I was already numb. It was mostly middle-class white women in high school or college, or young black women from inner-city Washington, D.C. A lot of the other young women were very nice. I didn't particularly like the religious aspect of the home, but other than that I thought they were very nice to us. But they very much had their own agenda, which was if you were white, they wanted your kid up for adoption. If you were black, they really didn't care.

When I was at the home for unwed mothers I had to see a social worker for a half an hour, once a week. The social worker mainly wanted to find out the birthfather's background in order to have all the data possible for matching my child with an adoptive family. I really got in the mode of thinking that I just wanted my child to have the best possible family, which I couldn't provide— and which they kept telling me I couldn't provide. So I highlighted all the things that were great in my family—all the people who were over-achievers. I didn't say anything about being Irish Catholic and having a number of alcoholics in the family. I kept hidden the fact that the birthfather had one sibling, his younger brother, who was mentally retarded. Once they found out that the birthfather went to Brown University, it got really ugly in a way. It seemed like the social workers clamped on to me like I was going to have the best baby in the bunch. They addressed my pregnancy with a lot of the "truisms" of Catholicism: that it was wrong to have a child out of marriage and therefore adoption was the best thing I could do for my child. I felt backed into a corner and shamed out of my child. The adoption was twenty-two years ago, and even after quite a few years of therapy, I still harbor a lot of resentment, mostly against people in institutions who think they know what is best for other people.

While I was pregnant, I was physically removed from my family, and the birthfather's parents became my caretakers. There is no doubt in my mind that they really cared a lot about me. There

> *"...I was so afraid that I didn't even ask really basic questions.*
> *I remember thinking that maybe because I wasn't married and the child was illegitimate that maybe legally she didn't belong to me."*

had always been a pretty strong bond between the two families, and the whole time I was at the home for unwed mothers they would take me out two or three times a week. They were at the hospital when I had my daughter. I had to have a cesarean, and when I was coming out of the anesthesia, I heard one of the nurses say to another, "They aren't her parents, they're the parents of the father." The nurses obviously felt like it was somehow disgusting that the birthfather's parents would be there. It was very strange. I felt like I sleepwalked through the whole experience. Most of it was a nightmare, but some parts of it were really nice; seeing my daughter was really nice. I remember the operating room that had these big windows, which I never expected. I looked out and saw this big field of tall grass and this blue, blue sky. I felt really good about my daughter being born and seeing her. I had to be adamant about seeing her because the hospital staff really didn't want me to see her.

Whether or not I could nurse my daughter was never discussed. I almost felt disenfranchised. This sounds stupid to me now, but I was so afraid. I don't know what I was afraid of—perhaps of having done something wrong and being punished? I don't know what it was, but I was so afraid that I didn't even ask really basic questions. I remember thinking that maybe because I wasn't married and the child was illegitimate that maybe legally she didn't belong to me. It was really nebulous, and nobody went out of their way to clear it up.

The birthfather's parents were crazy about the baby. They even talked to the obstetrician about keeping her—either me keeping her and them helping me financially, or them keeping her. The doctor said this would ruin my life. "She has got to get back to her old life or start a new life." I can't even explain what a horrible experience it was. The whole thing just felt so bittersweet—to be having my first child, and knowing that I wasn't going to be able to keep the child. Knowing that I was very young but feeling that I could do this if I got some help. Feeling like I had no right to ask my parents to help. I ended up feeling like I couldn't really ask the birthfather's parents to help me keep my daughter because I felt like it would have been an affront to my parents and that would hurt them even more. So I dropped the whole issue.

I stayed at the maternity home for three weeks after the birth. Every day I would go to the nursery and feed the baby her bottle. It just got to be too much of a strain because I knew that I was going to leave. So after a little more than two weeks, I called the birthfather's parents and asked them if they could get me. I felt like I had to leave because I couldn't take it anymore. However, before I left, we had my daughter baptized. I think it was on the same day I left, but I still don't remember. I don't remember that day at all. I guess my mind is just being kind to me.

I stayed in Washington, D.C., for another couple of months, mainly because I didn't want to go home and deal with my parents. Then I went back. When my parents met me at the airport they said, "We have a wonderful surprise for you. We are going to go on our vacation." So we drove to Arizona and saw the Grand Canyon. It was the first time—and the last— I ever saw it. I have this wonderful photograph of me standing in my coat with my long, straight hair, next to my mother. We are looking down into the Grand Canyon, and I remember feeling just like the Grand Canyon—vastly empty. I was thinking about my daughter constantly, and I was almost not aware of the passage of time. I didn't want time to go forward, I wanted it to go back— not back to before I was pregnant, but just back to when I had my daughter so I could be with her. My parents pushed me about returning to college, and I really didn't want to do anything. I wanted to be dead, but they pressed me, pressed me, and pressed me. They wanted me to become a useful member of society. I guess they thought I wasn't really good "merchandise" anymore. My parents suggested I go to secretarial school.

I felt like the pregnancy was my fault. However, I never felt ashamed, and that was the big difference between me and my parents. It didn't seem shameful to me. What I had a lot of trouble with at that particular time was that everybody in my generation was saying, "You don't have to get married, you can live together. Free love, do whatever you want." Except nobody wanted to deal with you if you had a child or if you got pregnant. If that happened you were just stupid. So I had trouble fitting in with people who were my contemporaries, and I had trouble fitting in with my parents. I just felt like I didn't fit in anywhere. During that first year and a half, I tried to kill myself twice. In order to fit, or in order just to keep going, I blocked it out.

Eleven years later when I was pregnant with my son, I felt really good. I thought, "Finally, I have done it the right way, and I am going to get to keep him. This is going to be great." When I had him, I was really happy at

"Practically, I know that there are children that need to be adopted. But if there was government help and help from religious organizations and philanthropies, I think that a lot more women would be able to keep their children."

first. Then, as he started changing and smiling at me as the weeks went by, it was very hard for me to deal with. Everything about my daughter just flooded back. I was totally in love with my son, Timothy, no doubt about it, but there was a strong resentment in me somehow that he wasn't her. I don't know how to explain it, but there were so many conflicting things going on in my head that it was very hard to deal with Timothy on a daily basis. Looking back on his infancy, I can see that I felt really resentful that not only did I lose my first child and can't remember the day I lost her, but in a lot of ways I lost my second child because I don't remember a lot from when Timothy was small. That's gone too.

After I had my son, I got horribly depressed about my daughter. In dealing with that depression I eventually began the search for her. I went back to Washington, D.C., which was the first time I had been back since I had given her up. I went back to the home for unwed mothers because I thought that maybe I could remember the day that I left. But I couldn't. I still don't remember.

When I found my daughter after a year of searching, I contacted her parents, but they didn't want to have too much to do with me. Her parents did write me a long letter and sent me pictures. It was pretty much, "Thank you very, very much for this wonderful, wonderful child. Now will you please, please go away again and never come back?" At the time, my daughter was 11 years old. When she graduated from high school, I sent her a card. I told her I would really like to know where she was going to college, not because I would try to come there and see her if she didn't want to see me, but because I always feel better knowing exactly where she is. It is like knowing where my son Timothy is. I don't understand why people find it so difficult to comprehend that I want to know where my child is. I don't need to know every second of every day, but I would like to know where she lives, what she is doing, and what is important to her. Over the last few years I have gotten worn down trying to keep in contact with her family, or with her. I know that you are always your parents' child, but I think there is a real strong agenda with a lot of adoptive parents that they can't deal with the birthparents because they feel threatened. They don't feel quite sure of the fact that they really are the child's parents.

Practically, I know that there are children that need to be adopted. But if there was government help and help from religious organizations and philanthropies, I think that a lot more women would be able to keep their children. That doesn't seem to be a real agenda in the world we live in. It is a sad thing, but I guess there is always going to be adoption. I would make it so that adoption is open. I would say live with an open adoption, or don't do it, because if you are adopting a child and you lose sight of the fact that this child has other parents, you are not dealing with the child's reality. Sooner or later it is going to hurt the child. I think it is going to hurt the adoptive parents as well because they are dealing with a reality gap too, just like I always have.

If a young pregnant woman came to me and asked my advice, and she was not able to marry, I would say either decide if you want to be a single mother or have an abortion. I would never in good conscience be able to recommend giving a child up for adoption. If you want to get religious about it and think that abortion is a death and that somebody has been killed, then a death is a final thing, and then you go on. With my daughter, I feel like she is being held hostage and it just goes on and on and on. Adoption has cost me too much. It has cost my son, and as far as I know, it has cost my daughter. It has cost my parents. It has cost my family for not having her in our lives. I think that we had a lot of really bad advice, and we were really naive.

I remember my mother always said that her father, who was all Irish and very dogmatic, said, "It isn't whether it is right or wrong, it is whether you can live with the consequences." Somehow I think the consequences should be a little bit more in line with what went down. I don't think having a child means that you should go through the rest of your life paying such a heavy emotional price.

I can't be around people who have adopted children, especially small girls. I have actually broken off friendships because people have adopted children. It is still too painful for me. I was really scared to talk about this because it just brings it all up again. I feel like I am always paying. For what? For caring? It seems like I'm paying a really heavy price for simply being human.

Mary Medlin

MELINDA KAHL

was adopted when she was two months old. Her adoptive parents divorced when she was 5, and she and her two adopted brothers were raised by their adoptive mother. Kahl says that all her life she wanted to find her birthparents, and when she was 19, she began her search. At age 21 she found her birthparents, who are cousins to each other. Kahl, 23, feels that something essential is missing from her life.

I always felt different from everybody because they had their birthparents and they grew up differently. I was always wondering what it would be like to have parents. I didn't fit in. There were a couple of boys that lived near our house. It seemed like they had a closer relationship with their parents. They could hug their parents, and it seemed like they had so much more understanding at home. They didn't have to worry about what they said or did. It is hard to put into words, probably because I feel like nobody wanted me when I was little.

Growing up, my adoptive mom used to hit us. She was an alcoholic, so there was physical and mental abuse. My adoptive dad didn't like girls. My adoptive mom tells me that he would never pick me up, but he would pick up my brothers. I grew up in a fancy house and went to a good school. Both of my parents worked, and they made good money. They bought us lots of presents, but I would rather have stayed with my birthmother and given up on the things that she wanted me to have. I would rather have stayed with my birthmother and had less, rather than be put with the high-class family who could afford all these things. I saw pictures of my birthmother after I was born and given up, pictures of their Christmases with Christmas trees. I could not look at those pictures, it made me so mad. If my birthmother could afford a tree, she could have kept me. It wouldn't have cost that much money. I would rather have stayed with her, even though she moved around a lot. I would not have minded.

My adoptive parents sent me to a psychiatrist when I was 5 years old. From then until I was 16, for nine years, I saw a psychiatrist. I never knew why. I always thought, "God, what's wrong with me? Why do I have to see these people?" They never helped me at all, they just made it worse. I don't feel like I know myself. That is one of the reasons that I contacted my birthparents. And now that I have contacted them, it is still just as bad. My birthfather is nice—he couldn't have wanted a daughter more. He said all his life he always wanted a daughter, and he never thought he would ever have one. He couldn't be more crazy about me. He wants me to come visit him in Minnesota, but I don't want to go. I tell myself it is because I have too much stuff to do around here. I don't want to be away from home for that long. I can think of all kinds of reasons, but really I think it's just my nervousness about going there, away from everything that is comfortable. If I go to Minnesota I won't know anybody. I'll be in a whole other state, and I will be totally alone. I can't be totally alone. I can never be totally alone. I would like to be with my birthfather, but I don't really know him. I have only spent about two weeks with him in my whole life, so he is still like a stranger. I want to feel like everybody else feels who grew up with their parents. But it is not like that.

Melinda Kahl

DAVID MENDOZA

is a birthfather who was 17 when his daughter was born and given up for adoption. After the adoption, he and the birthmother continued to see each other for about one year, despite her parents' objections. Mendoza eventually married another woman and had four more children. When he learned he could search for his adopted daughter, he began a long search that was hampered by his daughter's adoptive parents. Mendoza eventually met his daughter when she was 25 and continues to correspond with her. In addition to his biological children, Mendoza, 43, has two foster children living with his family.

When my girlfriend got pregnant, I didn't know I had rights as the father. I basically pleaded with her to let me have the baby, and I told her that my parents would help me. She said that since we were both from the same town it probably wouldn't work. My girlfriend's sister was pregnant, too. My friend and I were taking the sisters out, and they ended up getting pregnant at the same time. So if one sister were to keep the baby, or were to get married, both of them were. I think it was pressure they were getting from their parents.

When the baby was given up, it really hurt. It hurt that the baby was gone and that I thought I could cope with her giving up the baby, telling me this story about the baby having a better life. But there was nothing I could do about it, so I would just think about it. After a while, my girlfriend started feeling like I was blaming her for giving up the baby, and I guess I did. I tried not to. I tried to be understanding and everything. I knew the pressure was coming from her parents.

I've always remembered my daughter, especially on the day she was born. And as years went by, I would see kids that were about her age, and I started looking to see if I recognized her. A lot of times I saw kids, and I thought maybe my daughter could look like that. I was always looking.

While I was searching for my daughter, my wife kept me on a balanced level because it became an obsession sometimes. I could let other things go because I was searching so much. My wife would remind me to slow down and remember I've got other kids to take care of. I couldn't just leave my other children alone and start looking for my daughter.

Before I found my daughter, I found her adoptive mother and her new husband. I told them I just wanted to let my daughter know her heritage. I thought my daughter might have some fantasies about what happened, and I wanted to let her know I'm here and she has some roots. I wanted her to know she has family, brothers and sisters, and maybe she might be curious to know who they are. The adoptive mother's husband asked me a pointed question: "Why now? Since you gave her up?" I let him know that I wasn't the one that made the decision, and if it had been up to me, my daughter would have been with me. I told him how fortunate he was to be able to get my daughter in adoption. Then I asked, "Could you relay this message to her?" They said, "We stay out of her life, and we don't get involved." I felt, "Well, I guess that's it. I'll just let it ride and see what happens." I finally met my daughter when she was 25.

David Mendoza

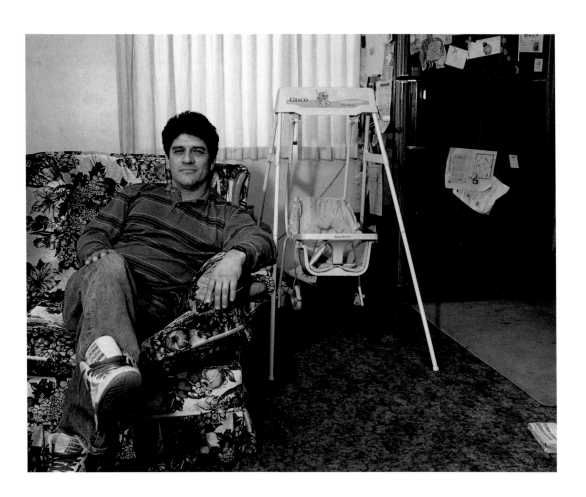

was 17 when she gave up her newborn son, Brandon Cox, for adoption. When he was 13, Warila was contacted by the adoption agency to provide medical and social information requested by the adoptive parents. Warila and the adoptive parents communicated by letter until Cox was 18, when they all met for the first time. Cox, 18, considers Warila, 36, a "close friend."

I was 16 when I became pregnant. Brandon's birthfather had deserted from the Army—it was during Vietnam—and I was on juvenile probation at the time and wasn't supposed to be seeing him. The pregnancy was proof that I broke my probation by continuing to see him. He left town, and I moved from the foster home back to my mother's house. I was about five months pregnant. My family wanted me to abort and fought head over heels about it. My probation officer wanted me to abort, but I didn't. My mother had made it pretty clear that I could not be at her home at all with my child. None of the adults in my life had really brought up adoption, except for my doctor, who had wanted me to do a private adoption. He became very angry with me when I went through the county for adoption. I figured that the county could screen. I didn't trust private adoptions at all. Up until the seventh month I planned to keep my son, but I couldn't figure out how to do it. It was 1971, food stamps weren't available, I couldn't figure out where to get the money. At 17, I was totally ignorant of adult things—how to open a checking account, how to pay taxes, how to get utilities turned on. I was really scared. The adult world seemed like a huge mystery.

When I made the decision to give up my son for adoption, I became resigned to it. At that point, I started believing that it was in my and the child's best interests, that the adoptive parents would be able to give this child a lot of things that I couldn't. My self-esteem became nonexistent. I felt that I didn't deserve my child knowing that there were people who couldn't have children who could probably be better parents. So I became resigned. I have blocked out a lot of things, but this last year a lot of things have come back. At the time, I enrolled at San Diego State College, and I was supposed to start three weeks before I delivered. The night before I was supposed to move into the dorm, I couldn't do it. I totally flipped out and became hysterical. I just could not take the pressure of having the child, giving the child up for adoption, and starting college. At the time, I felt that starting college was a betrayal of the baby, of pretending that he was never born.

After my parole officer brought me home from signing the birth papers, I cried for a long time. Then I stopped crying after I gave Brandon up for adoption. Now I choke up, but I won't sob, and I won't let the tears come. I guess I just stuff everything inside.

After the delivery, I felt a lot different from my friends overnight. It was like I was dealing with issues. All of a sudden I grew up, and it was hard to relate to the previous teenage antics that we all did. I started hanging out with older people. I had a lot of trouble being with young people my age.

For a while after the birth I always knew exactly how old Brandon was. I could tell you when he was eight months, two weeks, one day and three hours old. I went through a strange first

couple of months after the adoption. I would hear him crying, just for a second, and at the same time my milk would come out. To this day, I have always wondered if he was hungry at that time. I remember when he was five weeks old and already with his adoptive parents, I started panicking. I knew that something was wrong, and I have since found out that when he was five weeks old that he needed an emergency hernia repair. I tried to fantasize in my head what his bedroom looked like and what the parents were like. I scoped out every baby in the stores. I remember saying to my friends for the first two or three years that I felt I was handling it really well because I really didn't feel acute pain. Now I've come to think that I was totally numb about my own feelings. That numbness started wearing off after seven years.

Mother's Day was really hard. The birthdays were really hard. I tended to stay drunk on his birthdays. I remember when he turned 6. I was in New Mexico, and my aunt took me out that evening to one of the two places in town that you could go. It was a really tiny town, and we went out and I just got plastered. My aunt thought this was therapeutic for me because then I could let out my feelings, and that was one of the few times I cried. The next day she said, "Now that's over and done with, now get on with your life and forget it." I couldn't do that. People would say that to me a lot when my son was younger. "Why don't you just forget about him and have more children?" I couldn't. The caseworkers told me, "You'll get married, you'll have children, you'll forget, your life will be wonderful." Well, it didn't happen, I didn't forget. For a long time I thought that there must be something wrong with me because the experts said I should act a different way. I had a real hard time with my feelings. It has only been in the last year that I am becoming comfortable enough to feel again. This year has been tremendously healing.

When I met Brandon I had an immediate reaction that is hard to explain. Something inside me clicked, part of me I had lost so many years ago. I had often referred to the birth experience as though a part of me had died. The whole labor experience was devastating. I didn't want him to come out because as long as he was inside of me he was mine. So when we met, Brandon was 18. I had this feeling of completeness or wholeness, and that feeling has stayed. It was like part of my life suddenly made sense. I think that I would have known him anywhere.

I sometimes worry that Brandon might reject me. I am afraid to show him anger. I accidentally blew up—but not at him—last week, and it was a big deal. My roommate said he physically just snapped to attention, and his eyes got as big as saucers. I have been real afraid to show him any irritation at all because I am afraid he'll say, "Well, screw you," and go off and I would never see him again. But I don't think that will happen. The longer I am in this relationship with him, as time goes by, I think it is for life. I am sure there will be periods where we will both be angry with each other, just like in any family relationship. Right now, I believe my position is just to be here for him. I am not going anywhere. I don't care what this kid does in his life. He can get into as much trouble as he wants. He is not losing me. Even if he would end up in San Quentin, he will be the light of my life.

Seeing Brandon often brings up feelings that I wasn't aware that I had. They are way inside. Memories that have been blocked out for many years are starting to come back. This has to be healthy, because it's got to be really unhealthy to carry them around.

I think society views birthmothers as super-sluts. I don't think that a lot of the public realizes that they do it. I think that it is so automatic. A lot of people assumed that I didn't want the baby, which was the opposite from the truth. Another thing that really bothers me is that there seems to be a lot of fear of birthmothers. Fear that they are going to come in and steal their children. That drives me crazy. Hey folks, we gave up our children so that they could get better lives, and we aren't going to destroy anything that we have enabled them to have.

Debra Warila

Before I met Debbie I'd have my ups and downs. One day I was looking forward to meeting her, and the next day I wasn't so sure. But when I was reunited, for some reason I felt a sense of accomplishment—finally, after eighteen years I had accomplished something. We are alike. We think alike, and a lot of the things that we do are the same. It's really weird. We're avid coffee drinkers, and we smoke the same brand of cigarettes.

Debbie is my biological mom. Not to put her down, but I was raised for 18 years of my life without her. I look at Debbie as more of a close friend. But I think that was good. Open adoption may not be the best thing, I just don't know. If I was adopting a child, I don't know if I could stand an open adoption and having the birthparent coming over and influencing the child. And when it comes time for the birthparents and the biological child to be reunited, the adoptive parents should play a big role in that. They need to be a part of it.

Brandon Cox

CARL SCHURTER *was adopted at birth, and when he was 30 his adoptive mother gave him the names of his birthparents. Shortly thereafter, Schurter searched and found his birthfather. He found out he was the oldest of his father's nine children and the only one given up for adoption. Schurter, 36, is the youngest of four adopted children.*

Growing up, I felt like I was in a different place. I was just different. I would do things, and they were not pre-planned. They were just there, things inside me that were totally different from my family structure. I didn't know who I was. I was losing it. I had the feeling that I had to find out who I was to keep on surviving. I was thinking I was like the Earth losing a little bit of atmosphere, but I was losing a little bit of life at a time.

I got my birthfather's address, and I wrote a letter. It said, "Dear Sir, It is not my intention to cause you any grief or misfortune. I am just trying to seek my roots." I mailed the letter off, and it was a couple of weeks later that I got a reply from the guy. My adoptive mom said, "It is the Andrew guy on the phone." I answered, and he said, "Yeah, I'm him, but I don't understand this letter." And I said, "Well, did you know Virginia Smith?" And he said, "Yeah." And I said, "Well, did you knock her up?" And he said, "Yes." And I said, "Well, here I am." This heavy weight had been lifted. My birthfather then said, "Well, if you want any money, I don't have any," and he laughed. I said, "Don't worry about it, a rich dentist in California adopted me." He said, "Well, what do you want?" I said, "Well, I would kind of like to know who I am. I would like to meet you."

Then I talked to my birthfather's daughter several times before going to Louisiana to meet him. His daughter was going to meet me. So I got off the plane, and there were all these people around. I was looking around trying to find somebody, and everybody dissipated, and there was this one little short girl left over. She kept looking at me, saying, "Oh my God, oh my God." I was thinking, "Well what's the matter with you?" I was wearing this little French blue cap, which I later found out is what my birthfather wears when he goes to work. It was uncanny. We went to my birthfather's house and knocked on the door. The door opened, I walked in and shut the door. I saw this guy drinking. He kind of spit it out: I shocked him. I was wearing the same clothes, the same hat that he wore. He worked on a ship, and they said I looked like I was him twenty years earlier.

While I was visiting my birthfather, I kind of kept my distance. I carried a lot of guilt because I didn't want my adoptive parents to think that I was going to disown and replace them. Every day I phoned my adoptive family because I felt guilty. My half-sister by my birthfather said she loved me and all this stuff. I felt like I was somebody. They made a big deal over me. My natural grandma and grandpa figured I am the way I am because of them. I stayed in Louisiana for a year and a half. If I had been raised in Louisiana, it would've been a lot different because they were all crammed into one little shotgun house and their father was gone most of the time until the kids were a bit older. I have no regrets.

Carl Schurter

CAROL TEMPLE

was adopted at birth. After her adoptive parents died, Temple searched for and found her birthmother, who was 70 at the time. Temple was 51 when she found her. Although they correspond by letter and telephone, Temple's birthmother has resisted meeting her. Temple believes her birthmother has denied her daughter's existence to friends and family. Temple, 52, has a special devotion to animals, which she feels is related to her feelings of being adopted.

When I was growing up, adoption was definitely not a subject you discussed. I knew not to ask "those" questions. It was a feeling, a silence in the family, a secret. We were living with the secret, but never talked about it. Lots of times my friends would be talking about when they were born, and what it was like when their mothers were pregnant. I always felt separate from them at those times. I never had any of that information. I guess I never asked my adoptive mother about it. Once I did ask about my birthmother, and my adoptive mother acted defensive and hurt that I would even want information. I learned not to ask.

I remember my mother saying that the reason they adopted me was that my sister didn't have anybody. Everybody on my mother's side of the family and everybody on my father's side had natural children. It was only my mother and father that weren't able to have children. So they adopted my sister, who was considered different as far as the family was concerned. My mother said the reason they adopted another child was for her. I always felt I wasn't adopted for me—that there was another reason that was more important.

When I was a teenager, my adoptive mother used to say that her friend said, "All adopted children are bad seeds." I can remember that to this day. I can see the look on my adoptive mother's face. It was like I was a bad seed, but I didn't know why.

I always had the feeling that I was marching to a different beat. I know it sounds weird, but my friends all had some things I didn't have. They knew about their grandmothers. They knew about their cousins. They knew what they came from. I never knew any of those things. Once I knew I was adopted, it was like I didn't know anything. "What was my religion? What was my nationality? What was I? What did my mother look like? Would she look for me?"

I tried to explain it to my husband. He knows how long his mother was in labor with him, but he doesn't care. He can't understand how that could be important to me. But to a person who doesn't have that information, it is very important. Every time you go to a doctor or a dentist you are reminded that you're different because you don't have the information they're looking for. They are looking for your medical history, and you can't give it to them. How basic can you be? Here you are—you are you, but you don't know who you are because you don't know where you came from. But you know you came from something bad. Back in those days if you got pregnant—out of wedlock, for God's sake— that was criminal, both for the mother and the unborn child.

It's the secrets. I guess if I came away with anything about adoption, it was all the secrets. Everything was a secret. The birthmother was a secret. The adoptive parents were secretive. Then I became secretive because I didn't

"My love and devotion for animals has come from all this. I am so animal-oriented. It is a way not to have secrets. I take care of my animals like most people would take care of their children."

want people to know I was adopted. When I was older and I had to start giving that information out, I felt shame and powerlessness. When I was growing up I would hear some of the other mothers whisper, "Oh, she's adopted." So of course, the more it was whispered, the more awful I thought I was.

When I went to call my birthmother for the first time, my heart was literally in my throat. I had to dial that phone number, and all kinds of stuff went through my head. I was afraid to dial the number. I remember it took me the longest time to punch that last number in. I just didn't know what I was going to say. I didn't know what she was going to say. I thought, "What if she says she doesn't want to be around me?" There were a lot of feelings of rejection, a lot of feelings of fear. On the other hand, there was a lot of excitement because it sounded like my birthmother did want to talk to me. I didn't know what to call her. What do I call her? Mother? Do I call her by her first name? I didn't know what to call her. To this day I don't know what to call her.

Anyway, I dialed the number, and it rang and rang. Then someone answered the phone, it was this little tiny voice that said "Hello?" I thought, "This can't be her." So I said, "Is Virginia there?" I heard her just gasp, and she said, "Is this Carol?" I said, "Yes," and we both started crying. We talked for nearly three hours that day. The first five months were blissful. I was excited. But now that she doesn't seem interested in a person-to-person meeting, I am feeling rejected again, only even more so. Of course, I am reacting to it with anger. Now I feel like I am not going to call her—why won't she call me? I won't confront her about this situation because I'm afraid we won't have any relationship, so I just stew about it and hope she'll be more interested someday soon.

My love and devotion for animals has come from all this. I am so animal-oriented. It is a way not to have secrets. I take care of my animals like most people would take care of their children. Inside of me I don't feel that I can give to this mother who let me go. I can't give her the love because of these lost years. I've learned how to stuff away physical contact and love. I came from a family where there was very little touching. But with an animal, I can let that all out. I can put my arms around the animals, feel them, smell them, hold them, and they respond. It is so fulfilling. There is no rejection there—no secrets.

Carol Temple

LYNETTE KEIRN

was 2 years old when her birthparents were divorced. Keirn's birthmother remarried, and her second husband was abusive. When Keirn was 5, she and an older brother were placed in a foster home. Keirn was in several orphanages and foster homes until the age of 9, when she and her brother were adopted by separate families. Keirn joined the Navy when she was 17. Keirn's brother first contacted their birthmother, who subsequently contacted Keirn when she was 19.

Being in an orphanage felt like I didn't belong. I felt like I was just one person alone in the whole world. But you know, I grew used to it. I didn't really feel pain or joy or anything, I just started taking things as they came.

I was very glad to be away from the foster family because it was really terrible. They were physically and sexually abusive. Sometimes I just wanted to be dead. Every morning it was like a routine; I'd wake up and they would take me down to a cellar and they'd hit me. Every morning. After a while, I just kind of got used to it. By the time I was adopted, I had so much emptiness inside me I didn't want to know my adoptive parents. I didn't want them to feel any warmth for me, and I didn't feel any for them, at the time.

My adoptive family gave me stability. I might have come out worse. I might have started using drugs or hanging around with the wrong kind of people if I hadn't had them. Moving away to join the Navy was easy in the sense that I just wanted out. Afterwards, I kind of felt bad for the way I treated my adoptive family—not giving them the affection that they wanted and giving them such a hard time. Living with them made me grow up a lot. During the nine years that I spent with my adoptive family, I saw what it was to have somebody else in your life.

When I was 19, my birthmother called me. At first it didn't hit me. I thought, "Oh, I can deal with this." Everything was fine and I didn't feel anything. But three days later, I was walking around asking myself, "Who am I?" I felt totally invisible. It was weird not feeling that I belonged in life itself. Nothing seemed real. One night right after that, I woke up and I couldn't seem to remember my name. Things were slipping from my memory. Everything was slipping out of my grasp. I was afraid to get up and yell out the door for fear that nobody would hear me. I felt totally empty of everything. For the first time in my life, I talked to a psychologist. I talked to her for an hour, and she didn't help much. She told me, "Oh, you're a pillar of strength." And I said, "Gee, thanks." I never went back, but I felt better just talking about it.

I wouldn't change anything about my upbringing. Well, maybe little things— like I wouldn't have tolerated the treatment that I got in a couple of places. My upbringing made me stronger. I can deal with difficult situations at work that normally upset other people—like too much work. I can analyze and deal with emotion. There's a difference between being strong and closing things out. A complete difference. People often are afraid to look into themselves, but I'm not afraid to look into myself. Sometimes people are afraid of what they are going to be and what they are not going to be. I can look at things in a different light, feeling emotions, people and life. So I think in the long run I'll come out better.

Lynette Keirn

DELORES MENDIBLES

is the birthmother of Julie Palmer. Mendibles was 19 when she became pregnant. The father was married to another woman. Mendibles went to a home for unwed mothers, where her daughter was born and given up for adoption. She later married and had a second child, John. Mendibles' birthdaughter, Julie Palmer, was adopted into a family with three older biological sons. By the time Palmer was a teenager, she had a great deal of interest in meeting her birthparents. At 18 she began her search for her birthmother. When Palmer was 24 she had a daughter and gave her up for adoption. Two years later in 1990, Palmer and her birthmother were reunited. Palmer moved to California to live with her birthmother, 46, her half-brother, John, her mother's second husband, and his son. Currently, Palmer, 29, resides in Minnesota.

It was very difficult for me to contend with adopting out my daughter. The reason I made this decision was so that Ruth Ann [Julie's given name by her birthmother] would have a better life. She would have the food that she needed, and she would have good schooling, and she would be well taken care of. At that point I believed that I couldn't do that for Julie. That's the only thing that kept me going— knowing that I was doing the best for my daughter. That she would have a better life than if she was with me.

At first, when my daughter contacted me I was very excited and very nervous. I was feeling so many different emotions that it's hard to even explain what they were. I talked to the people at the adoption agency, and they said that they would forward a letter to me that Julie had written. I was very excited, but I didn't want the mail to come to my home because nobody knew about the adoption. So I rented a post office box, and I got her letters there. It was funny because I was working near the post office, so I'd wait in line before they opened. I'd get so excited just to check my mail. I'd read the letters and look at pictures out in the parking lot before I went to work. It was really something, a lot of emotions.

I called Julie on her 25th birthday. That was the first day I talked to her, May 18, 1989. Then I received more letters from her, and we talked on the telephone. I called her, and she called me. Julie and I discussed the adoption. I wasn't sure about telling my family, my brothers and sisters, about this. Then I decided, "Well, I'm going to tell my son first, and then I'll tell my husband, and then I'm going to tell the rest of my family." My mother didn't think I should tell my family after keeping it secret all these years, but I decided to do it anyway. I told my son, and then he talked to Julie on the telephone. He was all excited, and he was crying. He always wanted a sister or a brother, he's the only child. I told my husband, and he was thrilled. He understood, and there was no problem.

If I were pregnant now, in this day and age, I'm sure there would've been some way that I could've handled it, and I would've kept her. Now women can get better jobs—even 19-year olds. If I would've had a good job and if I could've financially kept her, I would have. My family wouldn't be a deterrent. Times have changed so much. There's a difference between my experience and when Julie gave her daughter up for adoption. She had options where she could see her child, and could visit with the people who adopted her child. I had none of those

> *"I feel like a whole person now, and I have also realized that people just don't understand how traumatic separation can be, even for a six-day-old infant, and how it affects your whole life."*

options, none. It was very cold and cut and dried.

Julie's tried to separate all these families. I think she shouldn't feel guilty for living with us or thinking, "If I talk to my mom in Minnesota, I'm going to make this mom feel bad." I say, "Don't. You have two moms. She took care of you, she raised you. She did her best, whatever that might be. Now you just have another family." I don't know if it's right or not, but I feel Julie could just blend in and be happy with the large family that she has.

Delores Mendibles

While growing up in my adoptive home, I felt very different from the rest of the family. I believe that those feelings were part of the reasons why it was hard to develop close relationships with my adoptive family. I was very rebellious and did not like to participate in family activities. Unfortunately, this put a strain on my relationships. My mom and I fought often, and I used the excuse that it was because I was different and that I was adopted. Ever since I searched for and found by birth family, so much has changed. It is exciting to have so much family and learn more about myself and my background, and that has filled a void I have had for a long time. I feel like a whole person now, and I have also realized that people just don't understand how traumatic separation can be, even for a six-day-old infant, and how it affects your whole life. This search was very emotional for everyone, but I often think of my adoptive mom, and how hard it must have been for her to "let me go" and have the strength to support my search and my move to California. I feel I have become much closer to my adoptive family since I "found myself."

I was really nervous about moving to California to live with my birthmother, but I was excited. Now I feel like I'd always been a part of the family. I am comfortable. It felt strange calling my birthmother "Mom" for the first time to her face. When I wrote to her I would say, "Dear Mom," but this was different. Meeting my birthmother filled a void that I always had. I felt complete as a person inside. Meeting my birthmother answered all the questions I had—like why I had curly hair, or who wore glasses, or who was left-handed. I didn't know any of that. When I found out all the things I had in common with my family, it made me feel like I belonged to something or someone.

Sometimes I wish I was forced to make a choice between families, because that would make it easier for me. I make sure I write enough to my adoptive parents so they don't think that I've deserted them. But yet, I'll call them and feel guilty for calling them, because I don't want to hurt my family here, even though they keep telling me I'm not. It's not as much of a hang-up as it was a couple of months ago.

When I became pregnant, I decided against abortion. I always respected my birthmother for the decision she made to not abort me or dump me in a trash can. There are a lot of things that could've happened. I knew inside that it was wrong for me. That's why I was hoping that I would have some other options come up. And that's what happened.

I ended up going back to Connecticut, where I was working as a nanny. I was calling around New York and Connecticut to find out about abortion, and I ended up calling this wrong number. I called Catholic Charities and they were very upset that I had asked about abortion. So then I told them, "Nobody's willing to help me. If you can help me, I won't do this. But there's nobody that's willing to help." I ended up in a maternity home and stayed there for six-and-a-half months. I won't recommend the home for a lot of people if they have another option. It was a very stressful time. I was alone most of the time. I had counseling for awhile, but my counselor ended up having a baby and didn't come back. So the last three or four months I was without counseling, except for the adoption worker. But I really wasn't interested in sharing what was going on with my life.

I do have regrets about not keeping my daughter. I know that what I did was right, and she's living a wonderful life. But sometimes I'm sad when I know that I gave up the only granddaughter that my birthmom has right now, or the only niece that my brother has. That bothers me sometimes, but what would have happened if I'd searched for my birthmother earlier? I may have never gotten pregnant. There are special times, like Christmas, or her birthday, or whenever I get pictures, when I miss all that. I'm missing seeing my daughter sit in the library and read, or swim, or take her first step. But I know she's happy, so that takes away a lot of the regret that I feel.

My advice to adopted people is not to let being adopted rule their lives. I think that's what happened with me. For awhile I was obsessed with it. I think I used being adopted for excuses sometimes.

Julie Palmer

ROBERT DUNCAN

was adopted at birth; however, he was never told by his adoptive parents. When Duncan was 48 his mother died, and he found an album of family papers that revealed he had been adopted. After searching, he learned that his birthmother was dead, but he did make contact with an older half-brother. Duncan is also an adoptive parent by marriage; as his wife's daughter was adopted during a previous marriage.

When I found out I was adopted, my feelings were very complex. To a certain degree, there was a sense of relief because I hadn't really fit in with my adoptive family. My mother was a very difficult person to get along with. On the other hand, it was a very bizarre feeling to wake up one day and find out that I was adopted. Suddenly a whole bunch of things that I'd always believed, such as things about my heritage, are not true. In effect, I had been through a lot of things in life and thought that I had myself pretty well figured out. Then all of a sudden I had a significant chunk of my identity withdrawn. What I had been led to believe wasn't true. A very peculiar experience. I was still in disbelief, so I went to two uncles who told me they had known that I was adopted for forty-nine years. It feels very strange when people know things about you that you don't even know about yourself.

I think adoption is born in dysfunction. It usually results from the adopted parents' inability to have children and the birthparents being unable to retain the child, usually for economic reasons. It ends up with the child being taken from the natural family and moved into an adoptive family. I know a few adoptees who say, "I love my adopted parents, and this is the best way to go." But by and large, it is not the natural order of things. Knowing the circumstances that my birthmother was living in, it was impossible for her to retain me. She had no choice but to relinquish me. I understand that. But given my choice, I would have probably preferred living with my birthmother in poverty instead of living with my adoptive parents.

I recognize that adoption has to occur in some cases. For example, if the parents of the child are killed in an automobile accident, then someone needs to take care of the child. My preference would be someone in the extended family. In some cultures that is the norm, and the relatives fight for the privilege. Other groups are very content to let the state take care of things. I think that is a mistake and is one of the first things I would change. I would limit adoption to a very few. The next thing I would do is try and provide resources to enable the families to stay together. I think that adoption is dysfunctional—you can have the nicest people in the world, and adoption still sucks. It is still a problem.

I am so conflicted now on abortion. It used to be simple. I believed that a woman had the right to make decisions about her own body. But now I look at it from a survivor's point of view. Had abortion been legal in the late 1930s, I probably wouldn't be here. Now I have gone back and rethought about it again and again. I'm honestly not sure where I stand.

I am not the only adoptee in my household. My wife's daughter was adopted during her previous marriage. My wife is a very nice person and is a good parent. She didn't adopt for the wrong reasons. But it still doesn't make things easier for our daughter, who is adopted. Going from being an adopted child to

> *"It seems to me that the focus ought to be on nurturing the adoptee to full identity. But the laws are set up more to protect adoptive parents than they are to help adoptees. I think this needs to be changed."*

an adoptive parent was a major shift for me. My relationship with my adopted daughter is evolving. It's common for adopted kids to keep a lot bundled up, and that was pretty much the case with my daughter. Now that I know I'm adopted, I've got doors open to me that allow me to say to my daughter, "Well, you probably feel like something is missing. You would probably like to walk into a room and see someone who looks like you." There are just some obvious connections that I have become aware of, and it gives me a totally different perspective.

One of the important decisions that I made in my own personal life during my first marriage was not to have children. Had I known that I was adopted, I would have made a different decision just to have someone in the world that I was related to directly, by blood.

One of the first reasons adoptees search for birthparents is just for information. It is necessary to help integrate the identity. In most cases, adoptive parents don't know the information either. It's like with our daughter—what we have is nonidentifying information. My wife doesn't know who her mother was, so she can't tell her. When I initiated the search for my parents, I went for nonidentifying information from the state of Illinois. I found out that they have a central search registry. I sent for the forms to put my name on the registry. I got the forms back, and they told me I had to appear personally before a court judge and have the court judge explain to me what it was that I was signing. The waiver would allow my birth relatives to contact me. Or, as an alternative, I could go to the county social services agency and have an adoption worker explain that to me. But if I did that, I would have to have it notarized there. I have a degree in social work myself. I am an adult, I have a responsible job, I have been in a war, yet they put me through all of these goddamn hoops just to tell me what the hell I was signing. There are only a couple of states in the United States that have open records at this point. And why? Who is it to protect? It sure as hell is not to help the adoptee. It seems to me that the focus ought to be on nurturing the adoptee to full identity. But the laws are set up more to protect adoptive parents than they are to help adoptees. I think this needs to be changed. At an absolute minimum, information about birthparents ought to be made available to the adoptee. The information ought to be sitting there, available to the adoptee as the adoptee needs it.

Open adoption is problematic because it means a million different things to a million different people. It's being enacted in many different ways, and there's no clear-cut thing called open adoption. One type of open adoption is that the birthparents get to pick who is going to adopt the child, and then the adoptive parents send pictures and tell them about the child. In that instance there is the risk of getting cut off at any point in time. That is not fair to a birthparent. It is not fair to an adoptee. So from birth to age 18, it's kind of confusing. I'm not sure what is right because it really has a lot to do with the individuals involved. But I think as a minimum, at age 18, the child should have all information made available. If they want to use it, that's fine. But it should all be available to the adoptees and to the birthparents. Just unseal everything at that point, and then they can work it out.

Adoptive parents make this big investment in a child—psychological, emotional, everything. They raise the child, and then this other person can walk into the room, and that other person might look just like the child and might act just like the child. All of a sudden there is this powerful attraction for the adopted child. So the reality seems to be that reunion scares a lot of adoptive parents to death, and that's why the laws are the way that they are. From the adoptees' point of view, most of them say, "Come on, as a parent, can't you love two kids? And do you necessarily favor one over the other? Can't I, as a child, love two parents?" And the reality is that a lot of children in our society now are faced with that situation anyway, with divorce being the way it is. They end up with two complete sets of parents, and sometimes more. So we have parallels everywhere. It's just around the adoption that it is really powerful. Why is it that so many adoptees feel a sense of guilt when searching out their birthparents. Isn't it coincidental that so many of them feel it? That is partly where I go back to my own experience. I had a situation where my adoptive family was so afraid of any sense of loss that they couldn't even tell me that I was adopted.

Robert Duncan

MARY KELLER *was adopted at birth into a family she describes as loving and religious. Keller was an only child, and although she feels she was raised "in the right family," she always wanted to know who her birthparents were. Keller was her birthmother's second child and was born when her mother was 18. Her birthmother had five children and married twice; she died when she was 52, years before Keller found her birth family in 1990. Keller, 45, sees being adopted and reunited as the most profound experience of her life.*

After years of searching on my own, I began going to Concerned United Birthparents [CUB] meetings, where I contacted a searcher, who found my birth family in fifteen minutes. I first found my grandmother Opal, who is an incredible, spunky, feisty, very bigoted Okie. I called her up and said, "My name is Mary Keller. I am calling from San Diego, and when I was born my name was Etta Opal Demoree." She was quiet for a minute, and then she said, "Oh, child, I always wondered what happened to you. Have you had a good life? Did you go to a good family?" I said, "Yes, I did." She said, "Well, good. You would have had a terrible time with my daughter, she wasn't very nice, and her husband was even worse. When are you going to come and see me?" I said, "I don't know. My husband and I will have to talk it over." We ended up going to visit that weekend. Opal told me I was born with a sexually transmitted disease and that they didn't think I was going to live. She told me this at dinner when we first met, and I just about choked. My birthmother had been violently abused by her father, including being stabbed and raped. And she did all kinds of horrible things to her own kids. The four children she did not relinquish (who all knew about me) were severely beaten and moved continuously throughout their childhoods.

It is ironic to me that almost everything I found out about my birthmother—from her profession to the way that I was conceived to her whole life—is so antithetical to the way I was raised, but it makes me feel less nuts. My whole life I've had real violent nightmares that didn't come out of my experience at all. Lots of knives, lots of stabbing, lots of intrusion, and I had this very quiet, gentle upbringing. Before my search, I had no thoughts about adoption being bad, even though it had quite a long negative impact on my life. Finding my birth family is a step that may have saved my life. I know that sounds overly dramatic, but I really felt so stressed out. To me, being adopted and being reunited has been the most profound experience of my life.

Connecting with my birth family has given me a sense of completion, answers to my questions, and the knowledge of my own story. Out of all the pain and shock of finding out my background has come the joy of finding my half-sister, with whom I share a very close relationship. Finding my half-sister has been affirming on every level I can think of. I finally feel like someone has shown my own story, and like it or not, it's mine. Knowing makes me feel like a part of the human race in a deeper way.

Mary Keller

LENI WILDFLOWER

is Cassie Wildflower's adoptive mother. Leni and her late husband, Paul, were friends with Cassie's birthmother in the late 1960s and cared for Cassie for the first few years of her life. Eventually, they agreed to continue taking care of Cassie only if they could adopt her. Cassie lived with her birthmother for a while when she was 16 and discovered that she was not the ideal parent she had fantasized about. After much struggle, Cassie feels she and her birthmother are now good friends. Leni, 45, and Cassie, 22, have also gone through many ups and downs in their relationship. Cassie now has a daughter of her own.

The circumstances surrounding our adopting Cassie were quite unusual. At the time my husband and I were in our 20s and had not thought the situation through thoroughly. We were involved in politics in the 1960s, and we got to know a woman who looked like she might be in trouble with the FBI. She asked us to help her have her baby, which we did. She came out to California with us, and we helped her get on welfare and find an obstetrician. At the last minute, I actually ended up in the delivery room when Cassie was born.

At that point, my husband, Paul, and I were not yet married, but we were living together. We assumed that we'd get married sometime down the road. Paul's mother was dying of cancer. Shortly after she died, Cassie's birthmom called and asked, "Will you take Cassie for a while?" The combination of being ready for a family and losing Paul's mother made us more open to taking Cassie. We took her for a summer, and at the end of the summer the birthmother came back and asked if we would keep Cassie for a couple of years. We told her, "Only if we can adopt her." In retrospect, I honestly had no idea what the ramifications of the whole adoption issue were. We adopted Cassie when she was 2 years old. A short time later I got pregnant with Jesse, who was born when Cassie was 3.

Our decision to adopt Cassie was based more on the politics of helping someone in need than on wanting a family. I think the birthmother thought she was giving her daughter, through adoption, to "big brother and sister, Leni and Paul" and that we'd all have some kind of relationship. We were not real clear about the whole arrangement. It's true that the birthmother was our friend and that she came in and out of our lives a few times. After we adopted Cassie, the birthmother came and went a total of three times. Each time, I got more upset about it. I felt there was a huge emotional charge around the visit, after which Cassie would cry for days. I felt like I was doing all the work and the birthmother was getting all the emotional goodies.

When Cassie was about 9, Paul and I made the decision to call her birthmother and tell her not to visit. It was very hard to do because I could sense her feeling of betrayal. Our therapist told us, "You adopted the daughter, not the mother. You take care of the daughter's needs, not the mother's." After the therapist said that, I understood what I needed to do. Later, the birthmother told me it was the best thing that I had ever said to her because it forced her to go on with her life. At the time, I told Cassie, "It's true that your mother gave birth to you, but I think a mother is the one who is with you all the time and who takes care of you and who slugs it out with you. I told your birthmom not

"Adoptive parents are the worst off in this whole triangle. Nobody likes us—birthparents, adoptees—we're like the stepmoms, the icky people who have all these false needs to raise these poor children."

to come back. If you want to see her later on, you can, but not now. Your mom is not going to come back." The next day, Cassie came out of her room and said, "You know what? If my birth-mom wants to be a mom, she's going to have to have her own children." I think it was a good decision all the way around, but it was hard to do, and we were unclear about it for several years. What Cassie needed to know was that her birthmom existed, that she could see her at some point, but she didn't need two competing moms.

When Paul and I adopted Cassie, the birthmother told us that Cassie's father was Puerto Rican. We talked to Cassie about being part Puerto Rican, the way the adoption people recommended. Later, when Cassie went to visit her birthmother, her birthmother told her, "You're not half Puerto Rican, you're half black. Your father was a Black Panther who was killed in Chicago." Cassie was furious. She would have been much better off knowing she was half black from the beginning.

I think that for children who are adopt-ed, the essential piece of information that nobody talks about, or even con-tradicts, is that somebody didn't want them. For whatever reasons, the birth-mother gave up her child. Adoptive par-ents write a fairy tale that the adopted child is everything they wanted, that they couldn't wait to get the child. While that may be true, they do the kids a disservice by not dealing with the pain and grief of the abandonment. One of the ways that people try to heal is by finding their birthparents. Seeing where they came from seems very workable, but the tragedy already hap-pened. Somebody didn't want them. Period. I don't think that most people deal with this fact, and when I've brought it up to birthparents, you can imagine their anger. They're walking around with so much grief and guilt, and they hardly want to be called child abandoners, especially by adoptive parents. Adoptive parents are the worst off in this whole triangle. Nobody likes us—birthparents, adoptees—we're like the stepmoms, the icky people who have all these false needs to raise these poor children. What people talk about now in open adoption is, "Your mom wanted you to have the best life, so she gave you to us." But somewhere along the line, the emotional reality doesn't jive with the story, and I think it makes kids crazy.

Many adopted kids have a sense of not belonging. One of the effects of this is that when the relationship with their adopted parents gets strained, the issue of not being genetically related comes into play. If you birth your child and that child acts like a heinous criminal, it's horrible, but there's a way in which you can stand it because it's your kid. If an adoptive kid begins acting out or doing things you find absolutely repulsive, the bonds begin to snap much more easily. You might never say it, but inside you think, "It's not my real kid." Adoptive parents always get the blame. The ones that really ought to be furious are the adoptive parents, because the kids feel that their birthparents are always out there, like a fairy godmother or godfather, and must be everything their adoptive parents aren't.

Since she was little, Cassie and I have grown enormously in our feeling for one another. This has been an ongoing struggle. It's been the Zen life lesson. As my husband once said to me, "The person Cassie needs as a parent is a combination of Buddha and General MacArthur." When Cassie went to visit

her birthmom at 16, her birthmom called me up, hysterical, and said, "I can't stand this kid, she acts just like I did." I couldn't stand Cassie either then, and she acted nothing like I did at 16.

I experienced a lot of guilt when Cassie would accuse me of loving her little brother, Jesse, more than her. I felt guilty because the truth was, I did. When I could finally say to Cassie, "You're right, I do," it was an enormous relief. Then we could begin to build a relationship. The reason I could finally say it was because I had come to love Cassie as much as Jesse, although as they were growing up it was much easier to love Jesse. He wasn't always testing my love. When my husband, Paul, died, I lost not only a companion but a partner in raising Cassie. Cassie went through a very difficult time after Paul died. She was 14 at the time, and very attached to him.

I don't think adoption, the way it is done in this country, is a functional institution. But what are you going to do, leave the kids in orphanages? If there was a neat solution, I'd probably be out lobbying for it right now. People give birth to children to meet emotional needs, which is already a problem, and when you bring in adoption, the problems get worse. Adoptive children feel different and spend their lives trying to fit into a shoe that doesn't fit.

If I had it to do over again, I am not sure that I would have adopted Cassie—or that she would have chosen us! I know this is not the conventional thing for an adoptive parent to say. But I'm also so grateful that it did happen, and that we did adopt her. I've learned so much from her and feel so much love for my adopted daughter. In retrospect, I wish someone had said to me at the time of adoption, "This child needs adults to act as parents and love her and care for her. She may never 'bond' with you. She may never be your daughter in the way you understand a mother-daughter relationship. But will you take her under these conditions?" If someone had said these words, I might have had more realistic expectations of what adoption meant. It might have spared both me and Cassie some needless heartache.

Leni Wildflower

I grew up knowing I was adopted. I have a little brother, Jesse, who is three years younger than me who isn't adopted, and I always felt like I was treated differently. Now I'm not sure I was. It always seemed like I was Daddy's girl and he was Mommy's boy. I always got along better with my adoptive father than my adoptive mother, so when my adoptive dad died when I was 14, I was stuck with my adoptive mom. I used to think that she was evil and that things would never work, but I feel differently now. I used to think it was because we were not genetically related, but now that I have more female friends my age, I think that most girls don't get along with their moms. I used to think she was just "anti-Cassie," but now I look back and appreciate in ways I never did before a lot of the things she did.

In school I had more trouble with the racial barrier than I did with being adopted. I first became aware of the racial difference when I looked at a picture of my family and noticed that I was a little bit darker than everyone else. The most difficult thing was having people not believe that Leni was my mother. People would ask, "Is that your mother?" So it always came up that I was adopted. I didn't think it was anybody's business, but it explained why we look so different. I get discriminated against from both sides. I get discriminated against by white people because I'm black and by black people because I'm part white. The racial situation isn't bad in California, but in Arizona, where I live now, it's really bad. A lot of my friends in Arizona are black, and when my adoptive mom came out to visit, they said, "That's your mom? She's white!" So I get the same thing from both sides. A few times when my little brother got at me, he used the word "nigger." I think he only said it three times, but it really sank in.

Being adopted, I think I was chosen, I really do. I think I could've had it a lot worse. I always wanted to grow up blonde-haired and blue-eyed with a white picket fence and a normal family with biological parents. But I think I'm a lot stronger and more able to cope with problems in my daily life now because of the strength I've gained from being in a different environment. I don't regret it for a minute. My adoptive mom might, but I don't. My adoptive family treated me really good. I had everything I needed. But when I was younger I wanted things different. Now that I'm older, I couldn't imagine myself with any other family. I really love my family.

Growing up, whenever my mom and I would get in a fight, I'd think, "I'm going to find my birthparents, and they'll come take me back. I'll convince them that they made a mistake and they love me and want me back." After meeting my birthmom, I'm not sure she's any less neurotic than my adoptive mom. My birthmother and my adoptive parents knew each other before I was born. When I was about a year old, my birthmother asked if they would keep me for a year and they said, "No problem." Then my birthmom came back and asked if they could keep me another year, and they thought about it for a while and said, "Only if we can adopt her."

My birthmom popped into my life a few times until my adoptive parents asked her not to. It was just too hard on me emotionally. We met again when I was 16, and we had a serious clash of personalities. We didn't get along at all. Then when I was about 18, my birthmom's grandmother died, and she asked me to come to the funeral. I went, and I spent the whole weekend dealing with the entire family. I took a friend along for emotional support, and it wasn't as bad as I thought it would be. Now my birthmom and I get along pretty good. I realized she wasn't the fantasy, the ultimate parent that I dreamed about in my mind.

I grew up thinking my father was a Puerto Rican man. We did some searching, and it turned out my father had been a Black Panther and had been murdered three months before I was born. Now I'm doing research on what this man was about, what he believed in. I think I have a lot of the same blood, and there's a lot of spirituality in the way I feel connected with my birthfather. Anytime I'm doing something I feel is morally wrong, I look up at the sky and am aware that I have two activist fathers looking down on me. I'm very aware of my birthfather's spirit, but I would love to have known him. I've been contemplating searching for his parents, but I'm leery of contacting them since I don't know how they'd react. I'm not quite sure if I'm ready or if they're ready.

I never thought about giving my daughter up for adoption. My birthmother was also adopted, and there was a tradition of adoption in her family. I decided that no matter what, the buck stops here. This tradition needs to change. I knew I wanted to have a baby, but I wasn't sure when. My pregnancy was kind of an accident, but as soon as I found out I was pregnant it was a planned pregnancy. There was no doubt in my mind that I would keep her. I even thought about adopting after I had her. When I get married I think I will adopt.

My birthmom and I get along well. She wants to be my mother, to step in and be Mom. I feel the blood connection between us, but I think of her as a special friend. It's hard because my birthmom gets offended if I don't send her Mother's Day cards, and Leni gets very hurt if I do. Sometimes I feel they're competing. It's also confusing when I go out with my birthmom and she says, "This is my daughter," because it's true and it's not. It feels strange.

Adoption is something that each individual has to deal with in his or her own way. Each family has its own barriers to overcome, and each person has insecurities. I can't say that one way would work for everybody, or that there's a certain way to do it. Children need to know they're adopted right from the get-go. Adoption is not a dirty word and is not a bad thing. It's important that when the child decides to find the birthparents that the adoptive family is supportive. It's important for people to know who they take after, who they look like, provided they are emotionally ready for it.

Cassie Wildflower

JOHN TURCO *is the son of two German nationals who had a brief affair while working in America. After their liaison ended, his birthmother discovered she was pregnant and gave John up for adoption. Turco's birthparents eventually returned to Germany and went their separate ways. About five years later, Turco's birthparents accidentally met in a German airport, and his birthfather learned that he was the father of a child in America. For the next twenty-five years, Turco's birthfather searched for him, and they finally met in 1990. Turco, 33, will travel to Europe to meet his birthmother, who has reluctantly agreed to meet him for the first time more than a year and a half after their first contact. His birthmother has four sons from her current marriage, but Turco will not be allowed to meet with them because they do not know about him.*

When my genetic father and I met, I had difficulty calling him my father. I have always called my adoptive parents "my parents," and it was strange to have someone else in my life and call him "Father." With all the effort and emotion that my birthfather had put into his search for me, he expected that I would embrace him as my father and we would live happily ever after. He envisioned that I would change my last name to his and move to Germany. Well, I have had a life for thirty years with a different name and a different family. I was very happy to meet him, but I was certainly not ready to change my name and move in with him. For me, our relationship had to go slowly, without a lot of pressure.

My adoptive parents have always been very supportive, and when I made the search for my birthparents they were always supportive. When I found I was actually going to make contact with my birthfather, my adoptive mother initially had fears. I think it was not as much of an issue for my adoptive father. It seems that for any woman who adopts a child, there is a fear in the back of her mind that the real parents are going to come and take the child away from her.

I felt embarrassed and strange when I first met my birthfather. I almost felt the need to apologize to my adoptive parents: "I'm sorry for putting you through this. I am sorry that this is upsetting to you, and I'm sorry that I was adopted. I am sorry that I am not your natural son." I can't think of any specific fantasies about my birthparents, but certainly, when I didn't know them, I could envision whatever I wanted. And then, suddenly I meet this guy and he is a real person, and there were things about my birthfather that I didn't like. I thought, think, "Gosh, he is part of me. He is part of what makes me up." It is really disorienting in a way. When you are raised with a particular parent, you learn to accept their faults. If I had been raised by my birthfather, I would just say, "Oh, Dad, you're a bigot, and just shut up." I found his bigotry really offensive. Certainly with my adoptive parents, I would just say, "Shut up." But when you are meeting your birthfather for the first time, all these little faults seem bigger.

After adoptees are a certain age I think it is ridiculous that they do not have access to information about their birthparents. Once you are an adult, you should be allowed to have that information if you want it. I understand the reasoning for the secrecy when you are a child. Why is it up to society to legislate this kind of stuff? It is a very personal, very private, and very emotional thing for the people involved.

John Turco

KAREN VEDDER

married when she was 19, and two-and-a-half years later she divorced her first husband because he physically abused her, and she feared he would abuse their son. Vedder became pregnant again when she was 23, but the birthfather disappeared. A few months later Vedder began dating an old boyfriend who was in the Merchant Marines. They moved to Texas, where he was stationed, and then married prior to the birth of her second child. Her husband did not want to raise two children by other men, so Vedder gave her second child, a girl, up for adoption, feeling she had no other choices. Vedder eventually had three sons with her second husband, however, she divorced him after thirteen years of marriage because he was abusive. Vedder first met her daughter, Gina, when Gina was 19. Vedder, 47, feels that being reunited with her daughter has been less than ideal.

My first husband physically abused me. Fearing for the safety of my son, I left him and went home and started working as a waitress. I got involved with a young man at the restaurant, and I got pregnant. We talked about getting married, and even though I wasn't in love with him, I felt that was my only choice. He moved to another state to find a job and new home for us. After a few weeks of talking on the phone, I didn't hear from him for a couple of days. I called his sister, where he was staying. She didn't know where he was. He disappeared. So there I was, approximately four months pregnant. I had come from a very strict Baptist background. I had sung in the choir and taught Sunday school. My divorce had already been a black mark on my name and my family's name. I felt my family couldn't handle my being single and pregnant.

I didn't know what to do or where to turn. When I found out I was pregnant, I went to the obstetrician who had delivered my son. He asked me what I was going to do. I told him I was going to get married, but when that fell apart, by the next time I went back for a checkup, I started to cry. I told the doctor I didn't know what I was going to do. He wrote a name on a Kleenex—we're talking 1964, and abortion was illegal—and he said, "Karen, I'm going to give you this name, but if you tell anybody I gave it to you, I'll deny it. But it is a name of someone who can help you." So I took the name and address, and I drove to Chicago, and I found the address—it was in a seedy part of town—and I drove around the block. I cried. I was a mess, and I didn't know what to do. I would like to say it's for some pro-life reason that I didn't go in there, but it was basically because of all the stories I had heard about botched abortions and women dying. My main concern was my son. I knew no one would love my son and raise him the way I would, and if I died on the table that wouldn't happen. So tearfully, I drove back home and proceeded with the pregnancy, still not knowing what I was going to do and not telling anybody. Nobody in my life knew I was pregnant, except for my doctor and this man who had taken off.

Then I met a high-school sweetheart, Pete, and told him of my dilemma, and he offered to take me to Houston, Texas, where I could relinquish the baby and no one would ever know. I made a lot of friends in Houston. I went to church there, and a lot of the church people had taken pity on my son and me, because Pete was usually gone to sea. Then I went in to have the baby. The whole time we had planned on just saying the baby had died, because people would wonder

"It is so wonderful when I'm in a room of birthmothers. None of us judges one another because we are the only ones who truly understand what the whole thing is about."

what happened to the baby. There was no way that I could have admitted I had relinquished the baby and that it wasn't Pete's baby because everyone thought we were a wonderful, cute young family from up North.

So I went in the hospital, and they induced labor. A nurse asked me if I was going to nurse the baby. I said, "No," and started to cry, and they put me out. The next thing I knew, I was awake and my baby was gone, and I didn't even know if I had a boy or a girl. It was an awful experience. I had no counseling at all. They discharged me from the hospital, and that was the end.

I went into pretend and denial. Pretend "It" didn't happen, because you don't want to upset everybody around you. We quit going to church. We told the few people that did call that the baby had died. It was pretend, denial, and lying. I started lying—I hate lying, and I want people to be honest and truthful with me—and for the next eighteen years I was a liar.

It was like somebody had sliced off a part of my life: a part of my body, a part of my being they grabbed from me. There was a big empty part that was missing, and yet I couldn't say to anyone, "Look, my arm is gone." I have a cousin who has diabetes. He lost his foot, and everybody is there sympathizing with him and feeling for him. I'm writing to him telling him how much I love him and feel for him. Nobody ever said anything to me about my missing part. When I look back on it, it was as if I was two different people: the perfect mom to my sons, submissive, obedient wife to my husband, and a shame-based woman living a lie, losing touch with my true feelings. Because of the lying, my feelings were never expressed.

Pete was there for the birth—not that he was supportive, but he was there. He came to visit me after the birth. I remember he got into bed with me and made overtures, like he wanted to fool around. I can remember almost being sick to my stomach thinking, "How can you do this to me at this time?" He had absolutely no feeling for my needs and what I was going through at that point.

Six weeks after I had the baby—at that point I didn't know whether it was a "her" or a "him,"—I went to get the mail. To this day I can remember that moment: the feelings, the scenery, almost the smells. That was twenty-three years ago. I went to get the mail with my son, and I was looking through it as I was walking back to the apartment. There was a postcard from the hospital where I had the baby, and it read, "Has your baby daughter had her shots yet?" That's when she became very real to me, because up to that point, when I couldn't put a gender on it, it was almost like a baby doll. Once I realized the baby was a girl and she was my daughter, I fell apart. I remember that I started crying, and when I got back into the apartment, I threw myself across the counter, and just sobbed and sobbed and sobbed.

Through the years, my grief would get so overbearing that I would cry out to my husband and let him know how hard this was on me. He wasn't very understanding, and I'm not sure he knew how to be. I would have fantasies about my daughter. I remember seeing the movie with Dustin Hoffman and Meryl Streep where she leaves and he raises the son. I remember her standing at the playground and watching her son. I would have fantasies of doing that. Standing and somehow knowing who my daughter was and just watch-ing her. When I would go to school functions, I would always look at the grade that my daughter would be in. I'd look at the outfits, look at the hairdos and wonder how my daughter was being cared for.

For eighteen years nobody in my family said anything to me about the relinquishment. The adoption was, I thought, a secret. I had sworn my mother to secrecy when I left Chicago because that's one of the reasons I did it that way—I didn't want that shame heaped on me or my family. So all these years I thought no one knew about it. But eighteen years after I relinquished my daughter, I was talking with my sister, and I could see something in her eyes. I asked, "Do you know about Houston?" And she said, "Yes." I have five brothers and sisters and my mother told them all, and yet nobody said anything all these years. Of course, that adds to the shame because you figure if nobody can talk about it, it must be incredibly shameful.

I'm still judged to this day. It wasn't too long ago that someone said to me they couldn't have done what I did. Someone who knows me very well and they still said that. So I'm still judged, and it's one reason why it is so wonderful when I'm in a room of birthmothers. None of us judges one another because we are the only ones who truly understand what the whole thing is about.

Karen Vedder

STEPHEN GONZALEZ

became a birthfather at 19, during his first year of college. His daughter was born in 1957, and she was given up for adoption at birth. Gonzalez later married a different woman, and they had a son before they divorced. He had two more children with another woman, but they never married. Gonzalez does not live with them, although he states he is quite close to the mother and the children, now aged 10 and 1. He currently lives with his mother and a nephew. Gonzalez, 54, searched and found his birthdaughter, Rebecca, now 35.

When I found my daughter, Rebecca, in January 1992, it was as if my life was complete for the first time since I was 19 years old. That was obvious to me, both in terms of my life decisions relating to my career and to relationships. I've felt incomplete, and I had never gone on to complete anything until I found my daughter. When I found her, I realized that my life had come full circle, and I did not care what happened to me after that.

When I found out my girlfriend was pregnant with Rebecca, I wanted to be with her and have the child and get married. At the same time, I wanted my independence and to be free of this "problem." I wanted to escape. I think that is characteristic of a style of mine— to resolve problems by escaping or ignoring them. This was the approach that my girlfriend and I were learning from our families on both sides. "Hide the problem away and ignore it," they said. Of course, both the birthmother and I knew this wouldn't work. Our families said to us, "Be rational and realistic. Getting married and keeping the child is not the right thing to do. Give up the child. That's what is best for the child, best for the mother, and best for you. Go on with your life." It was part of the American dream: "Go on, finish college, be a success." I felt angry at losing my daughter. Maybe anger at not having the courage to try and have a basic relationship with the birthmother. Anger at giving in to pressure from my parents and my girl-

friend's parents. Perhaps on an unconscious level, I saw being separated from my daughter as a punishment for not completing the original relationship with her birthmother.

Looking back on it, I'm ambivalent. I would have liked to have handled it differently, in a more mature way. I would have liked to work the relationship through, rather than just abandoning it. But on the other hand, I don't think the birthmother and I were particularly well matched.

It was always on my mind that I would eventually meet Rebecca. Maybe it comes from my Mexican-Catholic upbringing. The family is core, central to our lives. That bond between me and my daughter was always there, and all it needed was an opportunity to bring it to reality. Two things keyed my search. One, my daughter turned 30, and the other was the changing of society— there was more information available about searching.

I want people to understand something about birthfathers. I suspect there are macho guys who just impregnate women, walk off and never see them again. I believe on some level that goes on. But certainly, more men like myself wonder, "Do I get married, do I not get married?" In my case, I didn't. And the woman has the child—or at least in the 1950s and 1960s she did. I participated in the decision. I visited the birthmother when she was carrying the child,

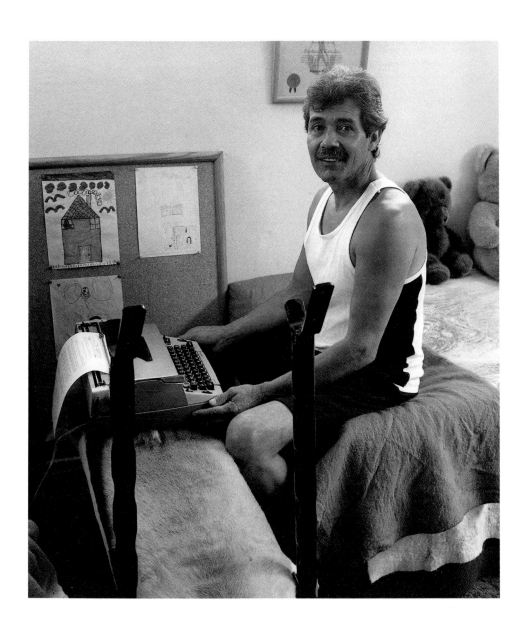

"I no longer adhere so closely to the cultural or Mexican ideal of what the male role is supposed to be."

even when we had to skirt the rules of the adoption agency and the home for unwed mothers. We were close, and I ended up bonding to the child. Every year on my daughter's birthday, I would think about her. On another level, I was always thinking about her. I know it's not the same as carrying the child, delivering it and then giving it up. It's like always being just beyond reach. Also, I buried a lot of my feelings, and that had to do with cultural sexual stereotypes.

For me, maturity means having a really strong economic base. The key to maturity is the ability to provide for yourself, and that starts with independence. Looking back on the time when we were deciding to give up Rebecca, I realize I didn't have the economic independence that would have allowed me the option of keeping the child or getting married. I had no job, no money. People kept asking, "What are you guys going to live on, especially with a child?" That didn't even enter my mind, but I wasn't thinking realistically then. In a way, I had no choice.

I've always been a bit of a rebel, going against the norm, but I don't think I could have taken on my school, all my classmates, my parents, all my family, and society by having a child out of wedlock. In the 1950s that would have been too much for me. Today, I would definitely do it. As a matter of fact, I'm doing it now.

My role as a birthfather has also changed as I've gotten older. I no longer adhere so closely to the cultural or Mexican ideal of what the male role is supposed to be. For example, the ideas that the father shouldn't change dirty diapers, or sing to the baby, or hold the baby, or be affectionate. That's ridiculous. Mothers are so busy now, especially if they are working. Raising a child is a full-time job, and the person raising the child needs help—relief in doing the dishes, the wash, changing the child, sitting with her, teaching her. All those activities are bisexual. The more you do these things, the more you overcome these cultural barriers.

Stephen Gonzalez

VICTORIA SMITH *was adopted at birth. At age 15, she became pregnant and, with the help of her adoptive parents, kept her son. When Smith was 22, she searched for her birthmother and found her in Australia. Later, she met her birthfather and several siblings. Smith, 28, works as a secretary in a law firm and lives with her 12-year-old son.*

When I was in the eighth grade I prayed that my mom, my birthmother, would be safe until I found her—that she would be alive. There were so many times I looked in the mirror, cried, and asked myself, "Who do I look like? Who am I?" I used to fantasize that I was Indian, or I was this, or I was that. I was told I was German, and I thought the worst. I thought, "I am all German, I could be related to Hitler." I imagined the worst-case scenario. I proceeded to read all about the Holocaust, thinking that I could have been related to some awful officer in Hitler's regime. I had these horrible thoughts, and I started to take it personally. In high school I read *The Diary of Anne Frank* and a lot of other books about how the Jews were persecuted, and I took that burden upon myself.

I used to fantasize that my mother had blonde hair and blue eyes. I had always wanted blue eyes because my eyes are so dark. Back then I never thought about my birthfather. There had been so many birthdays, Christmases, Easters, and other holidays—but mostly birthdays—where I would cry. I cried for my mother. I cried, "Where is she? Where is she?" My birthday is around Mother's Day, usually in the same week, and I remember in February of 1986 I prayed, "Lord, I don't care what you do. I don't care how you do it, but I want my mother back for my birthday." In April 1986 I found her, and I was with her for my 22nd birthday.

I went to Australia to meet my birthmother. When I was on the airplane, the closer I got to Sydney, the more critical of myself I became. I thought, "I hope I look like she wants me to. I hope I am the type of person that she would like. I hope she accepts me." I didn't care if she was a bag lady. I had this unconditional packet of love for her deep inside my heart. I would always love her, and although I was very excited, I was expecting the worst. As I was getting closer and closer, I became quite shaky. My dream was coming true. My deepest wish was coming true, my biggest hope, and I was very excited. I wrote this poem for my mother.

> I came through those doors
>   one sunny day
> to bring me to the place for which
>   I have always prayed.
> I wrapped my arms around my
>   mother's neck
> and we just stood there and
>   wept and wept.
> I wailed from my spirit way deep
>   down inside
> not ever wanting my loving mother
>   to leave my side.
> I could only cry for our mutual love
>   that seemed like a dream of a
>   beautiful descending dove.

I walked through the airport doors, waiting for my baggage to come down the chute, and it couldn't come quickly enough. In an international airport, you are not allowed in until you go through customs. The doors kept swinging open, and I could see the shape of three people standing there, looking in. I knew one was my mother as soon as I saw her outline. I couldn't see her. I just started crying and babbling to the person next to me, "I'm going to meet

"I think of it as one mother gave me life, and one gave me guidance. I couldn't have survived without one or the other."

my mom for the first time in my life!" I'm sure that these people were looking at me like I was crazy. I finally got to the point in customs where you declare all of your goods, and I couldn't get my luggage through the door fast enough. I put my arms around my mother's neck and cried a cry that I have never cried before or since. It was from my deepest emotions—I couldn't even imitate it, it was so intense. My mother was very silent, and she kept touching my face, and I just couldn't believe it was happening. It was very emotional.

After I found my mom, I felt normal. I felt at peace. I had always felt my fear: "Don't let me die until I find my mom, don't let her die until I find her." That day I actually felt I could've died. Nothing can compare with not knowing something so personal, so directly related to you, something you might never know.

A couple of years later, I found myself angry inside. I've never really expressed it to my birthmother. It was, "Why, why, why? Why couldn't she have worked it out? I did it. I was 15. How come she couldn't do it?" I just wanted to be with her. I wanted to know her. I realized that I could not get back anything that was lost. All I had was now and my future with her, and I had to make it the best.

When I was first pregnant with my son, his father would change his mind every other week about what he wanted to do. He knew that abortion was totally out of the question. He knew that he better not even mention the word to me because I am very pro-life because it hits home so personally for me. I thought I would be with my boyfriend forever. At 15, you think that you will be. My mother would drag me to

Children's Home Society for counseling every week, and they would proceed to tell me how selfish I was. How the odds were against me. How I would not be able to do this, that the only way out was to give this baby up for adoption. Every other month I would change my mind, so every other month they would give me choices of families. I think they were kind of telling me what I wanted to hear about people, or maybe they were truly trying to match up people with me. But I didn't want to give up my child. Deep down I didn't want to do it, but I was being so heavily pressured. At that time, I started inquiring about my birthmom. I already didn't know about the rest of my past. I didn't know my ancestry. I couldn't cope with more of not knowing. I have no doubt that I would have fallen apart if I had given up my son.

My adoptive parents gave their blessing to my search for my birthmother. I think my adoptive mom gave me the permission thinking that it would never happen. This is a closed adoption in California, and it won't happen. After I met my birthmother, my adoptive father was very happy for me. He actually met her and took her out for breakfast. My adoptive mom refused to meet her. I think it was too much reality for her to face, too much for her to bear. I think she was afraid that I was going to run off to Australia and never come back, that I would turn to my birthmother for everything and that I wouldn't look to her as my mother. My mom raised me, she cleaned up after me, she changed my diapers. She was there when I was sick. She was the one who put clothes on my back. She put me in good schools. She was there for me. I think of it as one mother gave me life, and one gave me guidance. I couldn't have survived without one or

the other. My adoptive mom got over it because over the years she saw that I was not going to take off.

My adoptive mom and I haven't had much communication because of my teenage pregnancy. I felt that I had really let her down and shamed the family. I had really hurt her so deeply that she couldn't find forgiveness. Finding my birthmother was just another blow, another big hurt that I had caused her to feel. Lately I have become closer to my adoptive mom. There is a lot more love, probably coming from my side for her. As I matured, we got along better, although my mom is not very communicative. At Thanksgiving she sent me a card, and inside she had taped this little saying, "Not flesh of my flesh, nor bone of my bone, but nevertheless still my own. Never forget for a single minute you weren't born under my heart, but in it." My adoptive mom is not like that. She has never sat me down and said, "You may not be mine by blood, but you're mine." It's hard for her to express her love. The card made me cry. I read it often because it means so much to me.

Victoria Smith

JIM SHINN fathered a son in 1970 when he was 17 years old. The child was given up for adoption at birth, and Shinn was not allowed to participate in this decision. From high school until his 30s, Shinn abused drugs and alcohol. When he began recovering from alcohol and drugs, he searched for his birthson and found him. Shinn's birthson visits him in the summertime and lives with his adoptive parents the rest of the year. Shinn was married for ten years and divorced and now has another son, who is 11 years old. Shinn, 39, works as a perinatal social worker.

My mom set up the family planning program in Imperial Valley, so I knew about contraception, and I was pretty responsible. I tried to be responsible. The night that our son was conceived I was using a condom, and the thing broke, and I was aware that it broke. I had the belief at that time that if you talk about pregnancy it will make the woman nervous and she will miss her period. So of course, I didn't talk about it. I also come from a family where you don't talk about stuff. That night when the condom broke, she knew it too, but we didn't talk about it. Then there was denial. We had been going together for a couple of years, but we broke up shortly after that.

It was probably four or five months later. I did not find out from the birthmother. She did not tell me, and several of my friends had already known that she was pregnant, but everybody tried to hide it from me. My new girlfriend told me that my ex-girlfriend was pregnant. I was in shock and very upset. I started crying real hard because I felt really bad. I was surprised because this was not something I ever expected to happen. This was something that happened in movies or to somebody else. I knew very few people who had gotten their girlfriends pregnant way back then, because if it did happen, generally it was really hush-hush. I felt a lot of guilt and a lot of shame.

I immediately told my parents about the pregnancy, and they were surprised. My mom was a little more supportive, but my dad's reaction was laughter. It wasn't until many years later I asked him how come he laughed in that situation. He told me that the week before I shared that news with him, he had given me a ride to college and told me how important it was to go out and have a large family and spread your seed. He was going on about the importance of a family and here, a week later, I come up with a child. He said, "Boy, you sure do work quick." I didn't see the humor of it at the time, I just thought my dad was being inappropriate. He was probably a little nervous too. The timing was not opportune because my dad and my mom were on the fritz at the time. Within a year they separated.

As soon as I found out, I immediately went back to my ex-girlfriend and tried to find out what my role was and what was going to happen. I don't remember very much about the dialogue. I don't remember whether I said she should get an abortion. I do remember that she had told her parents that we had only had sex one time and that the night we did have sex I had brought her some drinks and I had drugged her. She was basically just trying to survive because her dad was a six-foot-five sheriff from Alabama, so he was kind of an assertive guy. It did get to the point where her mother turned a shotgun on me.

There are so many things that hap-

"As a birthfather there is a lot of confusion.... I had a lot of conflicting things. People told me, 'You are lucky this is over.' But it was not over."

pened that made things worse. The first thing I had to deal with was the fact that her parents had been told that I had drugged her and had my way with her, so to speak. But the truth came out that this was not a one-time deal. But I didn't go around there anymore because they gave me a real strong message to stay away. Part of me was relieved because I didn't have to deal with this anymore. But the other part of it was the fact that I didn't really find out what happened with the child. I entered into a period of a lot of denial, some mourning and confusion.

As a birthfather there is a lot of confusion. If you have good support then confusion is minimized. I didn't have good support. I had a lot of conflicting things. People told me, "You are lucky this is over." But it was not over. That is bullshit—a rationalization that doesn't work. You've got to come to terms with the adoption eventually— which is what happened.

There was really a loss of self-esteem, and I felt bad. I felt I had brought on this shame. There was a lot of shame. I felt bad because I had screwed up this woman's life. I felt bad because I had done something wrong—my parents said you have sex in marriage and you do the right thing. Well, I was trying to do the right thing, but it wasn't really. No matter what I did, I still didn't feel like I was doing right. The right thing probably would have been to marry her and try to make a "decent woman" out of her, something like that. The birthmother didn't want to do that. At that time, she also had another boyfriend.

When this was happening, the way my friends wanted to support me was to just get high. I am a recovering drug addict and the way to deal with pain and loss was, "Let's get high." I dealt with my feelings by self-medicating. Nobody knew what to say. Nobody knew how to feel in this instance, so nobody talked about it. Even when my ex-girlfriend was pregnant, nobody told me about it.

I put the adoption away for years. Now I can look back and see, that was my grief, child loss, child death, abandonment, reunion, all those kinds of things. I didn't know where it was all coming from. That went on for ten years.

For me, I had to have permission to search for this child because as far as I knew, I had no rights to any information. It felt like I screwed up this woman's life and for me to ask anything about the baby was blasphemy. The last time I asked for information about the baby, I got two barrels of a shotgun pointed at me. Ten years later when I went to a Concerned United Birthparents [CUB] meeting, there were several birthmothers at the meeting, and they were glad to see me there. I had mixed feelings because a lot of birthmothers are so angry at the birthfathers. But I didn't really care. I started telling my story and sobbing, and they were crying with me. It was the first time anyone had ever really grieved with me. It was powerful. I said my piece and then sat back and listened for the rest of the meeting. They were talking about search and reunion and I was thinking, "You mean I can search if I want to? Oh, yes!" I went to CUB meetings for probably a year and a half before I made the decision to search.

I'm just tickled to have been reunited with my son because I could have gone without knowing him for life. There is a big hole that has now been filled. I have a really good relationship with his adoptive family, and they are very open. They are not really controlling like a lot of adoptive parents are. He lives with them most of the year, and he spends part of the summer with me and his birthmother.

My son's adoptive parents are the type of people I could have as friends. I like them, and they are not threatened. Their circumstances make it better because they also have biological kids. This adoption isn't based on the same type of loss like infertility. Theirs was just temporary. With many other adoptive parents, they're infertile, and this is all they got, and therefore they have to hold onto it, and they are really threatened.

Jim Shinn

SUSAN RINALDI WELDON *was adopted at birth. Her birthparents, who were unmarried when they gave her up for adoption, subsequently married and had four more children. In 1974, when Weldon was 16, she became pregnant, married, and, with the support of her adoptive family, kept her son. When she was 20, she and her adoptive mother searched for and found her birthparents. Weldon, 36, has become integrated into her birthparents' family and now feels she has two families.*

From the time I was too young to remember, my adoptive mom told me that we would find my birthmother some day. My adoptive mom had a friend who gave a baby up for adoption, and she went through that process with her. She stayed with her when she was pregnant and was with her when she gave up the baby. I guess that had a really significant impact on my adoptive mom. She spent the baby's first few birthdays with this friend.

My adoptive mom was almost 40 when she adopted me, after trying for a long time to have kids. She tells me that the day she took me home from the hospital, she made a promise to me and to my natural mother that she was just keeping me for awhile and that one day I would go back to my birthmother. So she just felt like I was hers temporarily. Somehow, there has always been this idea: you are going to find your mother. So finding my birthmother was never a startling revelation.

I have two families now. As far as I know there has been resistance from no one. My adoptive parents are supportive, and my birth family wanted it. My birthparents' kids had to get used to the idea, but now they are as much my brothers and sisters as anyone could be who didn't grow up together. It was scary meeting them and sitting with this family and looking around the table and having everyone looking alike. I used to think that who you were was basically a product of your environment. I thought you got certain things genetically but that your environment was really the big thing. I had to rethink that a little bit because we were raised by different people who obviously have different philosophies, and yet among the children, we all have some similarities that are hard for me to explain—our likes and dislikes, the way we react to situations, things we like to eat.

Meeting my birth family was like expanding my own family. My adoptive mom is excited about any opportunity to spend any time with my birth family. My brother and sisters, when they come here, she is their grandma because she is a whole generation older, and so it is just like an expanded family. There hasn't been any negative impact. My biological brother spent one summer at my house and one summer at my adoptive mom's. It is all a big family. I have added my birth family's name to my formal name. When I got divorced, I was trying to decide who I was going to be because I have had so many last names. I asked my adoptive mom how she would feel about it if I took my birth family's name as my last name, and she said, "I hoped that you would do that." That is something that only a unique person would say.

Susan Rinaldi Weldon

BARB HOLLES

is the adoptive mother of Amy Holles. Barb adopted Amy and another child, Paul, after she learned she was unable to conceive. When Amy was 8, Barb and her husband divorced. With the support of her adoptive mother, Amy searched for and found her birthparents when she was about 18. Amy's birthfather was living in Minnesota and her birthmother in Oregon. Currently, Barb, 49, and Amy, 22, both work in the same doctor's office.

When I was real young, I was told that adopted kids are special, so I was proud of it. After a while, when people made fun of me, I thought that was a bunch of hogwash. My older brother wanted to find his biological parents. I just assumed that was not the right thing to want, so I always said what I thought was expected of me. "No, this is fine. You're my mom and my dad, and I don't care to know." However, deep down I always had this goal to search for my parents when I turned 18. I always had this fantasy of going into a courtroom where the judge is sitting behind this huge desk. I'd say, " I want to know who my mom is." I just figured that I would do that at my first possible chance. But when that time came, I got real scared, and I didn't want to do it. I felt maybe just holding onto my dreams and my fantasies was better than having reality hit me. I was prepared for the fact that my birthmother might be a prostitute or just might have been too young. What I was most afraid of was that she wouldn't want to see me. One main reason I wanted to meet my birthmother was to thank her. I didn't really care to know the reasons why she gave me up. My adoptive grandmother always told me it takes a lot of love to give your kid up, and I believe that.

Meeting my birthparents has changed me. Now I know who I am. I feel real proud when I can tell people that I am Norwegian and Swedish. I know certain things about my birthparents: there are a lot of historical things in St. Paul that were built and established by members of my birth family way, way back. That feels really good; in a sense I feel complete. I definitely feel like there is a closure of some sort of hole that I have always felt. There was always something inside of me that wasn't filled, and by meeting my birthparents, I feel that it is completed. It has also taught me to not take family for granted. I didn't realize how much distance I had put between myself and my adoptive family until after I met my birthparents.

In the process of writing letters to my birthparents, I decided that I wanted my adoptive family to know about it, so I wrote a four-page letter to my family. I basically said, "This is what I am doing, and I want you to know about it. I am not doing it because I am not happy with any of you, and I'm not trying to find a new family. I'd like to share this with you, but if you don't want to be a part of it or hear about it, that's fine. But come to me if you want to know about it." It worked out really well; my family did call back and asked all about it. I have my problems with my adoptive family, but they are my family, and I love them. They are the ones who have seen me through everything, and I didn't want them to think that I was searching because I wasn't happy with them. It was a fun letter to write, and it felt good. I now have three mothers: my birthmother, my adoptive mother, and my stepmother. I want to get married to see if I can pull it off— have all of the mothers sitting in the front row in the same dress.

When I first met my birthparents, we

went through a phase where we didn't know what to call each other. My birthmother would write to me and say, "I don't really know who I am in your life. I am your friend, definitely, and I am your mother, but I don't really feel like a mom." I felt the same thing. I would tell her, "You're my mother. You brought me into this world, and you're the reason that I am here." But I don't feel like saying that she's my mom. It's always been friends, which is really good. My birthmother and I were pretty much in tune to each other as far as knowing how much space the other needed. My birthfather, on the other hand, was kind of tough. He wanted to make up for all of the past years, and he wanted to come in as Dad. He said he didn't want to, but in a way he did. And it was real hard because that's not what I wanted. My birthfather has been married, and they never had kids. Going around with him, he would introduce me to friends and say, "This is my daughter." I loved it that he was so proud of me.

When I first met them I was in a fantasy world for about five months. I was on top of the world. I thought, "This is incredible." I was accepted into the family. They took me on as if I had always been there. And in all my years of thinking about meeting my birthmother, I never dreamed I would get the chance to meet my birthfather. I became more secure and got more involved with things. I realized that I had a pretty good sense of humor and could make people laugh, and I flourished. The emphasis of my life was always on my birthparents or their parents. Anything I did those first four or five months was just centered around them.

Since then it has definitely changed. My birthfather and I have had problems. He told me all of these things. He had been in prison, he's an alcoholic, and he's not very responsible with his money. He bounces checks left and right and doesn't seem to take that too seriously. I always overlooked that and said, "Well, I don't care. I love and accept you. It's no big deal, and it doesn't matter to me." But moving six months after I had met them, I got to be away from everybody and reflect on everything that had been going on. I guess I realized that all of my dreams and fantasies weren't as wonderful as when I was going through them. The fantasy died off. The biggest problem that my birthfather and I have in our relationship is the fact that alcoholism has still gotten in the way. He has a lot of issues that he hasn't worked on yet. He likes to blame everyone, and he would blame me. Whereas with my birthmother, it is just a really good casual friendship. I know that I could call her anytime if I had something on my mind. It is the type of relationship where we can pick up after a month or two. We do not have to be constantly talking to each other, which is good.

I love my adoptive mother. Our relationship has changed so drastically over the last four or five years. I attribute it to finding my birthparents because my adoptive mother was so supportive of me. It brought us together. She was able to offer her support, and she was real genuine about her interest. We both grew up a lot. I take all of my dates to her. If she doesn't like them—get 'em out of here.

As a kid it's tough to know that you are adopted because it is hard to grasp why a mommy would want to give up her little girl. It's hard not to feel like there is something wrong with you. I have talked to people who are contemplating adopting children, and I tell them it is great. I always say that you really have to make sure that you reinforce to the kids that they are loved for who they are and they're not bad people. It is just so easy to get into thinking that you were just given up because you just weren't any good—that you weren't good enough.

Amy Holles

When the kids were young, we would talk about their being adopted. Paul, my son, would say, "I'm looking for my birthparents. When I'm 18, I'm going to look." Amy would say, "Not me, I never want to. That is really stupid." But Amy looked, and Paul hasn't.

When Amy first contacted her father, their relationship was pretty intense. He wanted to spend an awful lot of time with her, and some of the things that I heard about him and his background made me a little uncomfortable. Amy seemed, at that point, to be very defensive of the relationship, so we didn't talk about it a lot. I did meet the birthfather and got a six-page, single-spaced, typed letter where he told me how much he didn't like me because I reminded him of the nun at the unwed mothers' home who took the baby on the last day. At the time I felt that she was going to be very influenced and that she would change a lot. It was an environment that was real foreign to what I am used to, and I was feeling uncomfortable. My ex-husband was having a terrible time with the fact that Amy had found her birthfather, and we were getting a little tense because I was supporting her and he wasn't.

I remember someone saying to me, "It's really sad that you couldn't have one of your own." And I said, "What does that mean?" And they said, "Well, it's different if you have your own." I said, "How could you possibly know? You don't have any adopted ones." There is no difference. I don't have my own, but I can't imagine caring any more for one that I personally delivered than the two that I have.

Adoption is not seen as an option as much as it used to be, and I am not sure why. I think part of it is because society doesn't care if you have a baby and you are not married. Somehow adoption should be made more attractive. I work at Planned Parenthood, and a lot of times I bring up adoption as I am going through the options, and people say, "I never thought of that." It's like that's not a choice; you don't even hear it. There is a waiting list of twelve years, I think. It's crazy.

Barb Holles

Other Titles Available from NewSage Press

Family Portraits in Changing Times
by Helen Nestor

A Portrait of American Mothers & Daughters
by Raisa Fastman

Exposures: Women & Their Art
by Betty Ann Brown & Arlene Raven
Photographs by Kenna Love

Women & Work, Photographs and Personal Writings
by Maureen R. Michelson
Photographs edited by Maureen R. Michelson & Michael Dressler

The New Americans: Immigrant Life in Southern California
by Ulli Steltzer

Common Heroes: Facing a Life Threatening Illness
by Eric Blau, M.D.

Organizing for Our Lives: New Voices from Rural Communities
by Richard Steven Street
Interviews by Samuel Orozco

For a complete catalog, write to:
NewSage Press
825 N.E. 20th Ave.
Suite 150
Portland, OR 97232